Multiplayer Game Development with HTML5

Build fully-featured, highly interactive multiplayer games with HTML5

Rodrigo Silveira

BIRMINGHAM - MUMBAI

Multiplayer Game Development with HTML5

First published: May 2015

Production reference: 1260515

Published by Packt Publishing Ltd.
Livery Place
35 Livery Street
Birmingham B3 2PB, UK.

ISBN 978-1-78528-310-9

www.packtpub.com

Credits

Author
Rodrigo Silveira

Reviewers
Mahmoud Ben Hassine
Vinod Madigeri
Daniel Magliola

Commissioning Editor
Neil Alexander

Acquisition Editor
Sonali Vernekar

Content Development Editor
Arun Nadar

Technical Editor
Ryan Kochery

Copy Editor
Jasmine Nadar

Project Coordinator
Nikhil Nair

Proofreaders
Stephen Copestake
Safis Editing

Indexer
Rekha Nair

Graphics
Disha Haria
Jason Monteiro

Production Coordinator
Melwyn Dsa

Cover Work
Melwyn Dsa

About the Author

Rodrigo Silveira is a software engineer at Deseret Digital Media. There, he divides his time developing applications in PHP, JavaScript, and Java for Android. Some of his hobbies outside of work include blogging and recording educational videos about software development, learning about new technologies, and finding ways to push the Web forward.

Rodrigo received his bachelor's degree in computer science from Brigham Young University, Idaho, as well as an associate's degree in business management from LDS Business College in Salt Lake City, Utah.

His fascination for game development began in his early teenage years, and his skills grew as he discovered the power of a library subscription, a curious and willing mind, and supportive parents and friends.

Today, Rodrigo balances his time between the three great passions of his life—his family, software development, and video games (with the last two usually being mingled together).

I wish to thank my best friend and the love of my life, Lucimara, for supporting me in my many hobbies, her endless wisdom, and her contagious love of life. I also wish to thank my daughter, Samira, who makes each day shine brighter, as well as the latest addition to the team, my son, Juliano, who makes the world a better place by being an exciting part of it.

About the Reviewers

Mahmoud Ben Hassine is a software engineer with several years of experience in designing and developing Java-based solutions. For the last 10 years, he has worked in different industries (transport, telecommunication, and e-commerce) as a developer, team leader, consultant, and mentor.

Mahmoud is a passionate software developer who writes code for fun. In his spare time, he contributes to open source projects, writes technical articles, and gives talks about Java-related technologies.

> I would like to thank my family and my friends for their constant support, encouragement, and patience.

Vinod Madigeri is a software developer, game engineer, and technology enthusiast. He has worked with several game companies, and he recently graduated from the highest rated game development program at the University of Utah with a master's degree in entertainment arts and engineering.

> I would like to thank my professors at the entertainment arts and engineering program for their continuous support and dedication to expand my knowledge of game engineering.

Daniel Magliola has been writing code since he was 7 years old and games since he was 8. Through the years, he's dabbled in multiple technologies, such as GW-BASIC, C++, VB6, DirectX, C# and finally HTML5/JavaScript. These days you'll find him working at his start-up and experimenting to squeeze a few extra FPS out of JavaScript engines.

www.PacktPub.com

Support files, eBooks, discount offers, and more

For support files and downloads related to your book, please visit www.PacktPub.com.

Did you know that Packt offers eBook versions of every book published, with PDF and ePub files available? You can upgrade to the eBook version at www.PacktPub.com and as a print book customer, you are entitled to a discount on the eBook copy. Get in touch with us at service@packtpub.com for more details.

At www.PacktPub.com, you can also read a collection of free technical articles, sign up for a range of free newsletters and receive exclusive discounts and offers on Packt books and eBooks.

https://www2.packtpub.com/books/subscription/packtlib

Do you need instant solutions to your IT questions? PacktLib is Packt's online digital book library. Here, you can search, access, and read Packt's entire library of books.

Why subscribe?

- Fully searchable across every book published by Packt
- Copy and paste, print, and bookmark content
- On demand and accessible via a web browser

Free access for Packt account holders

If you have an account with Packt at www.PacktPub.com, you can use this to access PacktLib today and view 9 entirely free books. Simply use your login credentials for immediate access.

Table of Contents

Preface

Welcome to *Multiplayer Game Development with HTML5*. This book will teach you how to develop games that support interacting multiple players in the same game world, and how to perform network programming operations in order to implement such systems. It covers topics such as WebSockets and client-side and server-side game programming in JavaScript with Node.js, latency reduction techniques, and handling server queries from multiple users. We will accomplish this by walking you through the process of developing two actual multiplayer games from start to finish, and it will also teach you about various topics in HTML5 game development in the process. The aim of the book is to teach you to create game worlds for multiple players who want to compete or interact through the Internet using HTML5.

What this book covers

Chapter 1, *Getting Started with Multiplayer Game Programming*, introduces network programming, with emphasis on designing a multiplayer game. It illustrates the basic concepts of multiplayer game development by walking you through the creation of a real-time game of Tic Tac Toe.

Chapter 2, *Setting Up the Environment*, describes the current state of the art in the JavaScript development world, including JavaScript in the server through Node.js. It also describes the current techniques to manage the development cycle in JavaScript with workflow and resource management tools, such as Npm, Bower, Grunt, and more.

Chapter 3, *Feeding a Snake in Real Time*, takes an existing single-player Snake game and builds in the ability to play with multiple players in the same game world using the tools heretofore described. Concepts of lobby, rooms, matchmaking, and handling queries from users are also described and demonstrated, which add the functionality to the Snake game. The chapter introduces the most powerful and widely used WebSocket abstraction in the industry today — socket.io.

Chapter 4, Reducing Network Latency, teaches you techniques to reduce network latency in order to create a smooth playing experience. The most common among such techniques — client prediction — is demonstrated and incorporated into the Snake game that is described in the previous chapter. The game server code is also updated for the purpose of performance by introducing a second update loop.

Chapter 5, Leveraging the Bleeding Edge, describes the exciting opportunities that are found in game development on the web platform. It explains WebRTC, HTML5's gamepad, the fullscreen mode, and media capture APIs. Other promised and experimental technologies and APIs are also described here.

Chapter 6, Adding Security and Fair Play, covers common flaws and security vulnerabilities that are associated with network gaming. Here, common techniques are described and demonstrated, allowing you to develop games that provide a playing experience that is free from cheating.

What you need for this book

To use this book, you will need a working installation of Node.js and Npm, a modern web browser (such as Google Chrome 5.0, Firefox 3.5, Safari 5.0, or Internet Explorer 9.0 and their later versions), and a text editor or an integrated development environment (IDE). You will also need basic to intermediate JavaScript knowledge as well as some previous game programming experience, preferably in JavaScript and HTML5.

Who this book is for

This book is targeted at HTML5 game developers who can make basic single player games and would now like to learn how to incorporate multiplayer functionality in their HTML5 games as quickly as possible.

Conventions

In this book, you will find a number of text styles that distinguish between different kinds of information. Here are some examples of these styles and an explanation of their meaning.

Code words in text, database table names, folder names, filenames, file extensions, pathnames, dummy URLs, user input, and Twitter handles are shown as follows: " The first will be keyed with the value of `action` and the second will have a key of `data`."

A block of code is set as follows:

```
wss.on('connection', function connection(ws) {
    board.on(Board.events.PLAYER_CONNECTED, function(player) {
        wss.clients.forEach(function(client) {
            board.players.forEach(function(player) {
                client.send(makeMessage(events.outgoing.JOIN_GAME,
player));
```

When we wish to draw your attention to a particular part of a code block, the relevant lines or items are set in bold:

```
validator.isEmail('foo@bar.com'); //=> true
validator.isBase64(inStr);
validator.isHexColor(inStr);
validator.isJSON(inStr);
```

Any command-line input or output is written as follows:

```
npm install socket.io --save
npm install socket.io-client -save
```

 Warnings or important notes appear in a box like this.

 Tips and tricks appear like this.

Reader feedback

Feedback from our readers is always welcome. Let us know what you think about this book—what you liked or disliked. Reader feedback is important for us as it helps us develop titles that you will really get the most out of.

To send us general feedback, simply e-mail feedback@packtpub.com, and mention the book's title in the subject of your message.

If there is a topic that you have expertise in and you are interested in either writing or contributing to a book, see our author guide at www.packtpub.com/authors.

Customer support

Now that you are the proud owner of a Packt book, we have a number of things to help you to get the most from your purchase.

Downloading the example code

You can download the example code files from your account at `http://www.packtpub.com` for all the Packt Publishing books you have purchased. If you purchased this book elsewhere, you can visit `http://www.packtpub.com/support` and register to have the files e-mailed directly to you.

Downloading the color images of this book

We also provide you with a PDF file that has color images of the screenshots/diagrams used in this book. The color images will help you better understand the changes in the output. You can download this file from `https://www.packtpub.com/sites/default/files/downloads/3109OS_ Graphics.pdf`.

Errata

Although we have taken every care to ensure the accuracy of our content, mistakes do happen. If you find a mistake in one of our books—maybe a mistake in the text or the code—we would be grateful if you could report this to us. By doing so, you can save other readers from frustration and help us improve subsequent versions of this book. If you find any errata, please report them by visiting `http://www.packtpub.com/submit-errata`, selecting your book, clicking on the **Errata Submission Form** link, and entering the details of your errata. Once your errata are verified, your submission will be accepted and the errata will be uploaded to our website or added to any list of existing errata under the Errata section of that title.

To view the previously submitted errata, go to `https://www.packtpub.com/books/content/support` and enter the name of the book in the search field. The required information will appear under the **Errata** section.

Piracy

Piracy of copyrighted material on the Internet is an ongoing problem across all media. At Packt, we take the protection of our copyright and licenses very seriously. If you come across any illegal copies of our works in any form on the Internet, please provide us with the location address or website name immediately so that we can pursue a remedy.

Please contact us at copyright@packtpub.com with a link to the suspected pirated material.

We appreciate your help in protecting our authors and our ability to bring you valuable content.

Questions

If you have a problem with any aspect of this book, you can contact us at questions@packtpub.com, and we will do our best to address the problem.

1
Getting Started with Multiplayer Game Programming

If you're reading this book, chances are pretty good that you are already a game developer. That being the case, then you already know just how exciting it is to program your own games, either professionally or as a highly gratifying hobby that is very time-consuming. Now you're ready to take your game programming skills to the next level—that is, you're ready to implement multiplayer functionality into your JavaScript-based games.

In case you have already set out to create multiplayer games for the **Open Web Platform** using HTML5 and JavaScript, then you may have already come to realize that a personal desktop computer, laptop, or a mobile device is not particularly the most appropriate device to share with another human player for games in which two or more players share the same game world at the same time. Therefore, what is needed in order to create exciting multiplayer games with JavaScript is some form of networking technology.

In this chapter, we will discuss the following principles and concepts:

- The basics of networking and network programming paradigms
- Socket programming with HTML5
- Programming a game server and game clients
- Turn-based multiplayer games

Understanding the basics of networking

It is said that one cannot program games that make use of networking without first understanding all about the discipline of computer networking and network programming. Although having a deep understanding of any topic can be only beneficial to the person working on that topic, I don't believe that you must know everything there is to know about game networking in order to program some pretty fun and engaging multiplayer games. Saying that is the case is like saying that one needs to be a scholar of the Spanish language in order to cook a simple burrito. Thus, let us take a look at the most basic and fundamental concepts of networking. At the end of this section, you will know enough about computer networking to get started, and you will feel comfortable adding multiplayer aspects to your games.

One thing to keep in mind is that, even though networked games are not nearly as old as single-player games, computer networking is actually a very old and well-studied subject. Some of the earliest computer network systems date back to the 1950s. Though some of the techniques have improved over the years, the basic idea remains the same: two or more computers are connected together to establish communication between the machines. By communication, I mean data exchange, such as sending messages back and forth between the machines, or one of the machines only sends the data and the other only receives it.

With this brief introduction to the concept of networking, you are now grounded in the subject of networking, enough to know what is required to network your games—two or more computers that talk to each other as close to real time as possible.

By now, it should be clear how this simple concept makes it possible for us to connect multiple players into the same game world. In essence, we need a way to share the global game data among all the players who are connected to the game session, then continue to update each player about every other player. There are several different techniques that are commonly used to achieve this, but the two most common approaches are peer-to-peer and client-server. Both techniques present different opportunities, including advantages and disadvantages. In general, neither is particularly better than the other, but different situations and use cases may be better suited for one or the other technique.

Peer-to-peer networking

A simple way to connect players into the same virtual game world is through the peer-to-peer architecture. Although the name might suggest that only two peers ("nodes") are involved, by definition a peer-to-peer network system is one in which two or more nodes are connected directly to each other without a centralized system orchestrating the connection or information exchange.

On a typical peer-to-peer setup, each peer serves the same function as every other one — that is, they all consume the same data and share whatever data they produce so that others can stay synchronized. In the case of a peer-to-peer game, we can illustrate this architecture with a simple game of *Tic-tac-toe*.

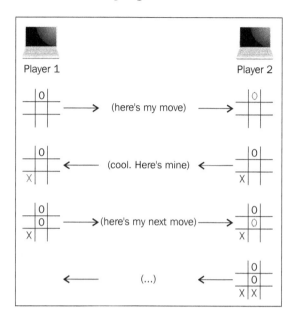

Once both the players have established a connection between themselves, whoever is starting the game makes a move by marking a cell on the game board. This information is relayed across the wire to the other peer, who is now aware of the decision made by his or her opponent, and can thus update their own game world. Once the second player receives the game's latest state that results from the first player's latest move, the second player is able to make a move of their own by checking some available space on the board. This information is then copied over to the first player who can update their own world and continue the process by making the next desired move.

The process goes on until one of the peers disconnects or the game ends as some condition that is based on the game's own business logic is met. In the case of the game of *Tic-tac-toe*, the game would end once one of the players has marked three spaces on the board forming a straight line or if all nine cells are filled, but neither player managed to connect three cells in a straight path.

Some of the benefits of peer-to-peer networked games are as follows:

- **Fast data transmission**: Here, the data goes directly to its intended target. In other architectures, the data could go to some centralized node first, then the central node (or the "server", as we'll see in the next section) contacts the other peer, sending the necessary updates.

- **Simpler setup**: You would only need to think about one instance of your game that, generally speaking, handles its own input, sends its input to other connected peers, and handles their output as input for its own system. This can be especially handy in turn-based games, for example, most board games such as *Tic-tac-toe*.

- **More reliability**: Here one peer that goes offline typically won't affect any of the other peers. However, in the simple case of a two-player game, if one of the players is unable to continue, the game will likely cease to be playable. Imagine, though, that the game in question has dozens or hundreds of connected peers. If a handful of them suddenly lose their Internet connection, the others can continue to play. However, if there is a server that is connecting all the nodes and the server goes down, then none of the other players will know how to talk to each other, and nobody will know what is going on.

On the other hand, some of the more obvious drawbacks of peer-to-peer architecture are as follows:

- **Incoming data cannot be trusted**: Here, you don't know for sure whether or not the sender modified the data. The data that is input into a game server will also suffer from the same challenge, but once the data is validated and broadcasted to all the other peers, you can be more confident that the data received by each peer from the server will have at least been sanitized and verified, and will be more credible.

- **Fault tolerance can be very low**: The opposite argument was made in the benefits' section of *Peer-to-peer networking* that we discussed previously; if enough players share the game world, one or more crashes won't make the game unplayable to the rest of the peers. Now, if we consider the many cases where any of the players that suddenly crash out of the game negatively affect the rest of the players, we can see how a server could easily recover from the crash.

- **Data duplication when broadcasting to other peers**: Imagine that your game is a simple 2D side scroller, and many other players are sharing that game world with you. Every time one of the players moves to the right, you receive the new (x, y) coordinates from that player, and you're able to update your own game world. Now, imagine that you move your player to the right by a very few pixels; you would have to send that data out to all of the other nodes in the system.

Overall, peer-to-peer is a very powerful networking architecture and is still widely used by many games in the industry. Since current peer-to-peer web technologies are still in their infancy, most JavaScript-powered games today do not make use of peer-to-peer networking. For this and other reasons that should become apparent soon, we will focus the rest of the book almost exclusively on the other popular networking paradigm, namely, the client-server architecture.

Client-server networking

The idea behind the **client-server networking** architecture is very simple. If you squint your eyes hard enough, you can almost see a peer-to-peer graph. The most obvious difference between them, is that, instead of every node being an equal peer, one of the nodes is special. That is, instead of every node connecting to every other node, every node (*client*) connects to a main centralized node called the *server*.

While the concept of a client-server network seems clear enough, perhaps a simple metaphor might make it easier for you to understand the role of each type of node in this network format as well as differentiate it from peer-to-peer (*McConnell, Steve, (2004) Code Complete., Microsoft Press*). In a peer-to-peer network, you can think of it as a group of friends (*peers*) having a conversation at a party. They all have access to all the other peers involved in the conversation and can talk to them directly. On the other hand, a client-server network can be viewed as a group of friends having dinner at a restaurant. If a client of the restaurant wishes to order a certain item from the menu, he or she must talk to the waiter, who is the only person in that group of people with access to the desired products and the ability to serve the products to the clients.

In short, the server is in charge of providing data and services to one or more clients. In the context of game development, the most common scenario is when two or more clients connect to the same server; the server will keep track of the game as well as the distributed players. Thus, if two players are to exchange information that is only pertinent to the two of them, the communication will go from the first player to and through the server and will end up at the other end with the second player.

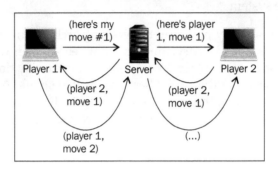

Following the example of the two players involved in a game of *Tic-tac-toe* that we looked at in the section about peer-to-peer, we can see how similar the flow of events is on a client-server model. Again, the main difference is that players are unaware of each other and only know what the server tells them.

While you can very easily mimic a peer-to-peer model by using a server to merely connect the two players, most often the server is used much more actively than that. There are two ways to engage the server in a networked game, namely in an authoritative and a non-authoritative way. That is to say, you can have the enforcement of the game's logic strictly in the server, or you can have the clients handle the game logic, input validation, and so on. Today, most games using the client-server architecture actually use a hybrid of the two (authoritative and non-authoritative servers, which we'll discuss later in the book). For all intents and purposes, however, the server's purpose in life is to receive input from each of the clients and distribute that input throughout the pool of connected clients.

Now, regardless of whether you decide to go with an authoritative server instead of a non-authoritative one, you will notice that one of challenges with a client-server game is that you will need to program both ends of the stack. You will have to do this even if your clients do nothing more than take input from the user, forward it to the server, and render whatever data they receive from the server; if your game server does nothing more than forward the input that it receives from each client to every other client, you will still need to write a game client and a game server.

We will discuss game clients and servers later in the chapter. For now, all we really need to know is that these two components are what set this networking model apart from peer-to-peer.

Some of the benefits of client-server networked games are as follows:

- **Separation of concerns**: If you know anything about software development, you know that this is something you should always aim for. That is, good, maintainable software is written as discrete components where each does one "thing", and it is done well. Writing individual specialized components lets you focus on performing one individual task at a time, making your game easier to design, code, test, reason, and maintain.

- **Centralization**: While this can be argued against as well as in favor of, having one central place through which all communication must flow makes it easier to manage such communication, enforce any required rules, control access, and so forth.

- **Less work for the client**: Instead of having a client (peer) in charge of taking input from the user as well as other peers, validating all the input, sharing data among other peers, rendering the game, and so on, the client can focus on only doing a few of these things, allowing the server to offload some of this work. This is particularly handy when we talk about mobile gaming, and how much subtle divisions of labor can impact the overall player experience. For example, imagine a game where 10 players are engaged in the same game world. In a peer-to-peer setup, every time one player takes an action, he or she would need to send that action to nine other players (in other words, there would need to be nine network calls, boiling down to more mobile data usage). On the other hand, on a client-server configuration, one player would only need to send his or her action to one of the peers, that is, the server, who would then be responsible for sending that data to the remaining nine players.

Common drawbacks of client-server architectures, whether or not the server is authoritative, are as follows:

- **Communication takes longer to propagate**: In the very best possible scenario imaginable, every message sent from the first player to the second player would take twice as long to be delivered as compared to a peer-to-peer connection. That is, the message would be first sent from the first player to the server and then from the server to the second player. There are many techniques that are used today to solve the latency problem faced in this scenario, some of which we will discuss in much more depth later in *Chapter 4, Reducing Network Latency*. However, the underlying dilemma will always be there.

- **More complexity due to more moving parts**: It doesn't really matter how you slice the pizza; the more code you need to write (and trust me, when you build two separate modules for a game, you will write more code), the greater your mental model will have to be. While much of your code can be reused between the client and the server (especially if you use well-established programming techniques, such as object-oriented programming), at the end of the day, you need to manage a greater level of complexity.

- **Single point of failure and network congestion**: Up until now, we have mostly discussed the case where only a handful of players participate in the same game. However, the more common case is that a handful of groups of players play different games at the same time.

Using the same example of the two-player game of *Tic-tac-toe*, imagine that there are thousands of players facing each other in single games. In a peer-to-peer setup, once a couple of players have directly paired off, it is as though there are no other players enjoying that game. The only thing to keep these two players from continuing their game is their own connection with each other.

On the other hand, if the same thousands of players are connected to each other through a server sitting between the two, then two singled out players might notice severe delays between messages because the server is so busy handling all of the messages from and to all of the other people playing isolated games. Worse yet, these two players now need to worry about maintaining their own connection with each other through the server, but they also hope that the server's connection between them and their opponent will remain active.

All in all, many of the challenges involved in client-server networking are well studied and understood, and many of the problems you're likely to face during your multiplayer game development will already have been solved by someone else. Client-server is a very popular and powerful game networking model, and the required technology for it, which is available to us through HTML5 and JavaScript, is well developed and widely supported.

Networking protocols – UDP and TCP

By discussing some of the ways in which your players can talk to each other across some form of network, we have yet only skimmed over how that communication is actually done. Let us then describe what protocols are and how they apply to networking and, more importantly, multiplayer game development.

The word protocol can be defined as *a set of conventions* or a *detailed plan of a procedure* [Citation [Def. 3,4]. (n.d.). In Merriam Webster Online, Retrieved February 12, 2015, from `http://www.merriam-webster.com/dictionary/protocol`]. In computer networking, a protocol describes to the receiver of a message how the data is organized so that it can be decoded. For example, imagine that you have a multiplayer beat 'em up game, and you want to tell the game server that your player just issued a kick command and moved 3 units to the left. What exactly do you send to the server? Do you send a string with a value of "kick", followed by the number 3? Otherwise, do you send the number first, followed by a capitalized letter "K", indicating that the action taken was a kick? The point I'm trying to make is that, without a well-understood and agreed-upon protocol, it is impossible to successfully and predictably communicate with another computer.

The two networking protocols that we'll discuss in the section, and that are also the two most widely used protocols in multiplayer networked games, are the **Transmission Control Protocol (TCP)** and the **User Datagram Protocol (UDP)**. Both protocols provide communication services between clients in a network system. In simple terms, they are protocols that allow us to send and receive packets of data in such a way that the data can be identified and interpreted in a predictable way.

When data is sent through TCP, the application running in the source machine first establishes a connection with the destination machine. Once a connection has been established, data is transmitted in packets in such a way that the receiving application can then put the data back together in the appropriate order. TCP also provides built-in error checking mechanisms so that, if a packet is lost, the target application can notify the sender application, and any missing packets are sent again until the entire message is received.

In short, TCP is a connection-based protocol that guarantees the delivery of the full data in the correct order. Use cases where this behavior is desirable are all around us. When you download a game from a web server, for example, you want to make sure that the data comes in correctly. You want to be sure that your game assets will be properly and completely downloaded before your users start playing your game. While this guarantee of delivery may sound very reassuring, it can also be thought of as a slow process, which, as we'll see briefly, may sometimes be more important than knowing that the data will arrive in full.

In contrast, UDP transmits packets of data (called *datagrams*) without the use of a pre-established connection. The main goal of the protocol is to be a very fast and frictionless way of sending data towards some target application. In essence, you can think of UDP as the brave employees who dress up as their company's mascot and stand outside their store waving a large banner in the hope that at least some of the people driving by will see them and give them their business.

While at first, UDP may seem like a reckless protocol, the use cases that make UDP so desirable and effective includes the many situations when you care more about speed than missing packets a few times, getting duplicate packets, or getting them out of order. You may also want to choose UDP over TCP when you don't care about the reply from the receiver. With TCP, whether or not you need some form of confirmation or reply from the receiver of your message, it will still take the time to reply back to you, at least acknowledging that the message was received. Sometimes, you may not care whether or not the server received the data.

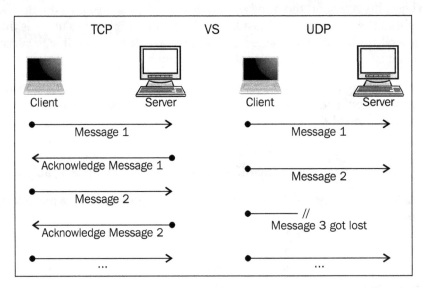

A more concrete example of a scenario where UDP is a far better choice over TCP is when you need a heartbeat from the client letting the server know if the player is still there. If you need to let your server know that the session is still active every so often, and you don't care if one of the heartbeats get lost every now and again, then it would be wise to use UDP. In short, for any data that is not mission-critical and you can afford to lose, UDP might be the best option.

In closing, keep in mind that, just as peer-to-peer and client-server models can be built side by side, and in the same way your game server can be a hybrid of authoritative and non-authoritative, there is absolutely no reason why your multiplayer games should only use TCP or UDP. Use whichever protocol a particular situation calls for.

Network sockets

There is one other protocol that we'll cover very briefly, but only so that you can see the need for network sockets in game development. As a JavaScript programmer, you are doubtlessly familiar with **Hypertext Transfer Protocol** (**HTTP**). This is the protocol in the application layer that web browsers use to fetch your games from a Web server.

While HTTP is a great protocol to reliably retrieve documents from web servers, it was not designed to be used in real-time games; therefore, it is not ideal for this purpose. The way HTTP works is very simple: a client sends a request to a server, which then returns a response back to the client. The response includes a completion status code, indicating to the client that the request is either in process, needs to be forwarded to another address, or is finished successfully or erroneously (*Hypertext Transfer Protocol (HTTP/1.1): Authentication, (June 1999).* `https://tools.ietf.org/html/rfc7235`)

There are a handful of things to note about HTTP that will make it clear that a better protocol is needed for real-time communication between the client and server. Firstly, after each response is received by the requester, the connection is closed. Thus, before making each and every request, a new connection must be established with the server. Most of the time, an HTTP request will be sent through TCP, which, as we've seen, can be slow, relatively speaking.

Secondly, HTTP is by design a stateless protocol. This means that, every time you request a resource from a server, the server has no idea who you are and what is the context of the request. (It doesn't know whether this is your first request ever or if you're a frequent requester.) A common solution to this problem is to include a unique string with every HTTP request that the server keeps track of, and can thus provide information about each individual client on an ongoing basis. You may recognize this as a standard *session*. The major downside with this solution, at least with regard to real-time gaming, is that mapping a session cookie to the user's session takes additional time.

Finally, the major factor that makes HTTP unsuitable for multiplayer game programming is that the communication is one way—only the client can connect to the server, and the server replies back through the same connection. In other words, the game client can tell the game server that a punch command has been entered by the user, but the game server cannot pass that information along to other clients. Think of it like a vending machine. As a client of the machine, we can request specific items that we wish to buy. We formalize this request by inserting money into the vending machine, and then we press the appropriate button.

Under no circumstance will a vending machine issue commands to a person standing nearby. That would be like waiting for a vending machine to dispense food, expecting people to deposit the money inside it afterwards.

The answer to this lack of functionality in HTTP is pretty straightforward. A network socket is an endpoint in a connection that allows for two-way communication between the client and the server. Think of it more like a telephone call, rather than a vending machine. During a telephone call, either party can say whatever they want at any given time. Most importantly, the connection between both parties remains open throughout the duration of the conversation, making the communication process highly efficient.

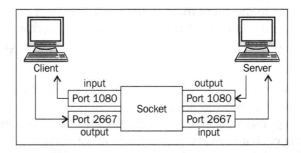

WebSocket is a protocol built on top of TCP, allowing web-based applications to have two-way communication with a server (*The WebSocket Protocol, (December 2011)*. `http://tools.ietf.org/html/rfc6455 RFC 6455`). The way a WebSocket is created consists of several steps, including a protocol upgrade from HTTP to WebSocket. Thankfully, all of the heavy lifting is done behind the scenes by the browser and JavaScript, as we'll see in the next section. For now, the key takeaway here is that with a TCP socket (yes, there are other types of socket including UDP sockets), we can reliably communicate with a server, and the server can talk back to us as per the need.

Socket programming in JavaScript

Let's now bring the conversation about network connections, protocols, and sockets to a close by talking about the tools — JavaScript and WebSockets — that bring everything together, allowing us to program awesome multiplayer games in the language of the open Web.

The WebSocket protocol

Modern browsers and other JavaScript runtime environments have implemented the WebSocket protocol in JavaScript. Don't make the mistake of thinking that just because we can create WebSocket objects in JavaScript, WebSockets are part of JavaScript. The standard that defines the WebSocket protocol is language-agnostic and can be implemented in any programming language. Thus, before you start to deploy your JavaScript games that make use of WebSockets, ensure that the environment that will run your game uses an implementation of the **ECMA** standard that also implements WebSockets. In other words, not all browsers will know what to do when you ask for a WebSocket connection.

For the most part, though, the latest versions, as of this writing, of the most popular browsers today (namely, Google Chrome, Safari, Mozilla Firefox, Opera, and Internet Explorer) implement the current latest revision of RFC 6455. Previous versions of WebSockets (such as protocol version - 76, 7, or 10) are slowly being deprecated and have been removed by some of the previously mentioned browsers.

 Probably the most confusing thing about the WebSocket protocol is the way each version of the protocol is named. The very first draft (which dates back to 2010), was named *draft-hixie-thewebsocketprotocol-75*. The next version was named *draft-hixie-thewebsocketprotocol-76*. Some people refer to these versions as 75 and 76, which can be quite confusing, especially since the fourth version of the protocol is named *draft-ietf-hybi-thewebsocketprotocol-07*, which is named in the draft as WebSocket Version 7. The current version of the protocol (*RFC 6455*) is 13.

Let us take a quick look at the programming interface (API) that we'll use within our JavaScript code to interact with a WebSocket server. Keep in mind that we'll need to write both the JavaScript clients that use WebSockets to consume data as well as the WebSocket server, which uses WebSockets but plays the role of the server. The difference between the two will become apparent as we go over some examples.

Creating a client-side WebSocket

The following code snippet creates a new object of type WebSocket that connects the client to some backend server. The constructor takes two parameters; the first is required and represents the URL where the WebSocket server is running and expecting connections. The second URL, which we won't make use of in this book, is an optional list of sub-protocols that the server may implement.

```
var socket = new WebSocket('ws://www.game-domain.com');
```

Although this one line of code may seem simple and harmless enough, here are a few things to keep in mind:

- We are no longer in HTTP territory. The address to your WebSocket server now starts with `ws://` instead of `http://`. Similarly, when we work with secure (encrypted) sockets, we would specify the server's URL as `wss://`, just like in `https://`.

- It may seem obvious to you, but a common pitfall that those getting started with WebSockets fall into is that, before you can establish a connection with the previous code, you need a WebSocket server running at that domain.

- WebSockets implement the same-origin security model. As you may have already seen with other HTML5 features, the same-origin policy states that you can only access a resource through JavaScript if both the client and the server are in the same domain.

For those who are not familiar with the same-domain (also known as the **same-origin**) policy, the three things that constitute a domain, in this context, are the protocol, host, and port of the resource being accessed. In the previous example, the protocol, host, and port number were, respectively ws (and not wss, http, or ssh), www.game-domain. com (any sub-domain, such as game-domain.com or beta.game-domain.com would violate the same-origin policy), and 80 (by default, WebSocket connects to port 80, and port 443 when it uses wss).

Since the server in the previous example binds to port 80, we don't need to explicitly specify the port number. However, had the server been configured to run on a different port, say 2667, then the URL string would need to include a colon followed by the port number that would need to be placed at the end of the host name, such as ws://www.game-domain.com:2667.

As with everything else in JavaScript, WebSocket instances attempt to connect to the backend server asynchronously. Thus, you should not attempt to issue commands on your newly created socket until you're sure that the server has connected; otherwise, JavaScript will throw an error that may crash your entire game. This can be done by registering a callback function on the socket's onopen event as follows:

```
var socket = new WebSocket('ws://www.game-domain.com');
socket.onopen = function(event) {
    // socket ready to send and receive data
};
```

Once the socket is ready to send and receive data, you can send messages to the server by calling the socket object's `send` method, which takes a string as the message to be sent.

```
// Assuming a connection was previously established
socket.send('Hello, WebSocket world!');
```

Most often, however, you will want to send more meaningful data to the server, such as objects, arrays, and other data structures that have more meaning on their own. In these cases, we can simply serialize our data as JSON strings.

```
var player = {
    nickname: 'Juju',
    team: 'Blue'
};

socket.send(JSON.stringify(player));
```

Now, the server can receive that message and work with it as the same object structure that the client sent it, by running it through the parse method of the JSON object.

```
var player = JSON.parse(event.data);
player.name === 'Juju'; // true
player.team === 'Blue'; // true
player.id === undefined; // true
```

If you look at the previous example closely, you will notice that we extract the message that is sent through the socket from the `data` attribute of some event object. Where did that event object come from, you ask? Good question! The way we receive messages from the socket is the same on both the client and server sides of the socket. We must simply register a callback function on the socket's `onmessage` event, and the callback will be invoked whenever a new message is received. The argument passed into the callback function will contain an attribute named data, which will contain the raw string object with the message that was sent.

```
socket.onmessage = function(event) {
    event instanceof MessageEvent; // true

    var msg = JSON.parse(event.data);
};
```

Downloading the example code

You can download the example code files from your account at http://www.packtpub.com for all the Packt Publishing books you have purchased. If you purchased this book elsewhere, you can visit http://www.packtpub.com/support and register to have the files e-mailed directly to you

Other events on the socket object on which you can register callbacks include `onerror`, which is triggered whenever an error related to the socket occurs, and `onclose`, which is triggered whenever the state of the socket changes to *CLOSED*; in other words, whenever the server closes the connection with the client for any reason or the connected client closes its connection.

As mentioned previously, the socket object will also have a property called `readyState`, which behaves in a similar manner to the equally-named attribute in AJAX objects (or more appropriately, `XMLHttpRequest` objects). This attribute represents the current state of the connection and can have one of four values at any point in time. This value is an unsigned integer between 0 and 3, inclusive of both the numbers. For clarity, there are four accompanying constants on the WebSocket class that map to the four numerical values of the instance's `readyState` attribute. The constants are as follows:

- `WebSocket.CONNECTING`: This has a value of 0 and means that the connection between the client and the server has not yet been established.

- `WebSocket.OPEN`: This has a value of 1 and means that the connection between the client and the server is open and ready for use. Whenever the object's `readyState` attribute changes from CONNECTING to OPEN, which will only happen once in the object's life cycle, the `onopen` callback will be invoked.

- `WebSocket.CLOSING`: This has a value of 2 and means that the connection is being closed.

- `WebSocket.CLOSED`: This has a value of 3 and means that the connection is now closed (or could not be opened to begin with).

Once the `readyState` has changed to a new value, it will never return to a previous state in the same instance of the socket object. Thus, if a socket object is CLOSING or has already become *CLOSED*, it will never *OPEN* again. In this case, you would need a new instance of WebSocket if you would like to continue to communicate with the server.

To summarize, let us bring together the simple WebSocket API features that we discussed previously and create a convenient function that simplifies data serialization, error checking, and error handling when communicating with the game server:

```
function sendMsg(socket, data) {
    if (socket.readyState === WebSocket.OPEN) {
        socket.send(JSON.stringify(data));

        return true;
    }
```

```
    return false;
};
```

Game clients

Earlier in the chapter, we talked about the architecture of a multiplayer game that was based on the client-server pattern. Since this is the approach we will take for the games that we'll be developing throughout the book, let us define some of the main roles that the game client will fulfill.

From a higher level, a game client will be the interface between the human player and the rest of the game universe (which includes the game server and other human players who are connected to it). Thus, the game client will be in charge of taking input from the player, communicating this to the server, receive any further instructions and information from the server, and then render the final output to the human player again. Depending on the type of game server used (we'll discuss this in the next section and in future chapters), the client can be more sophisticated than just an input application that renders static data received from the server. For example, the client could very well simulate what the game server will do and present the result of this simulation to the user while the server performs the real calculations and tells the results to the client. The biggest selling point of this technique is that the game would seem a lot more dynamic and real-time to the user since the client responds to input almost instantly.

Game servers

The game server is primarily responsible for connecting all the players to the same game world and keeping the communication going between them. However as you will soon realize, there may be cases where you will want the server to be more sophisticated than a routing application. For example, just because one of the players is telling the server to inform the other participants that the game is over, and the player sending the message is the winner, we may still want to confirm the information before deciding that the game is in fact over.

With this idea in mind, we can label the game server as being of one of the two kinds: authoritative or non-authoritative. In an authoritative game server, the game's logic is actually running in memory (although it normally doesn't render any graphical output like the game clients certainly will) all the time. As each client reports the information to the server by sending messages through its corresponding socket, the server updates the current game state and sends the updates back to all of the players, including the original sender. This way we can be more certain that any data coming from the server has been verified and is accurate.

In a non-authoritative server, the clients take on a much more involved part in the game logic enforcement, which gives the client a lot more trust. As suggested previously, what we can do is take the best of both worlds and create a mix of both the techniques. What we will do in this book is have a strictly authoritative server, but clients that are smart and can do some of the work on their own. Since the server has the ultimate say in the game, however, any messages received by clients from the server are considered as the ultimate truth and supersede any conclusions it came to on its own.

Putting it all together – Tic-tac-toe

Before we go crazy with our new knowledge about networking, WebSockets, and multiplayer game architecture, let us apply these principles in the simplest way possible by creating a very exciting networked game of *Tic-tac-toe*. We will use plain WebSockets to communicate with the server, which we'll write in pure JavaScript. Since this JavaScript is going to be run in a server environment, we will use **Node. js** (refer to https://nodejs.org/), which you may or may not be familiar with at this point. Do not worry too much about the details specific to Node.js just yet. We have dedicated a whole chapter just to getting started with Node.js and its associated ecosystem. For now, try to focus on the networking aspects of this game.

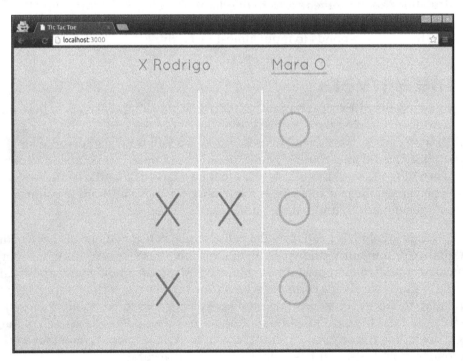

Surely, you are familiar with *Tic-tac-toe*. Two players take turns marking a single square on a 9x9 grid, and whoever marks three spaces on the board with the same mark such that a straight line is formed either horizontally, vertically, or diagonally wins. If all nine squares are marked and the previously mentioned rule is not fulfilled, then the game ends in a draw.

Node.js – the center of the universe

As promised, we will discuss Node.js in great depth in the next chapter. For now, just know that Node.js is a fundamental part of our development strategy since the entire server will be written in Node, and all other supporting tools will take advantage of Node's environment. The setup that we'll use for this first demo game contains three main parts, namely, the **web server**, the **game server**, and the **client files** (where the game client resides).

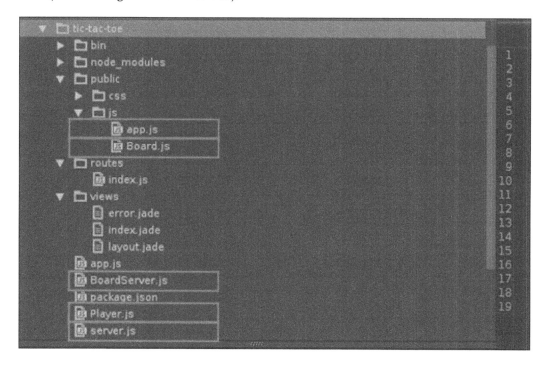

There are six main files that we need to worry about for now. The rest of them are automatically generated by Node.js and related tooling. As for our six scripts, this is what each of them does.

The /Player.js class

This is a very simple class that is intended mostly to describe what is expected by both the game client and the server.

```
/**
 *
 * @param {number} id
 * @param {string} label
 * @param {string} name
 * @constructor
 */
var Player = function(id, label, name) {
    this.id = id;
    this.label = label;
    this.name = name;
};


module.exports = Player;
```

The last line will be explained in more detail when we talk about the basics of Node.js. For now, what you need to know it is that it makes the `Player` class available to the server code as well as the client code that is sent to the browser.

In addition, we could very well just use an object literal throughout the game in order to represent what we're abstracting away as a `player` object. We could even use an array with those three values, where the order of each element would represent what the element is. While we're at it, we could even use a comma-separated string to represent all the three values.

As you can see, the slight verbosity incurred here by creating a whole new class just to store three simple values makes it easier to read the code, as we now know the contract that is established by the game when it asks for a `Player`. It will expect attributes named `id`, `label`, and `name` to be present there.

In this case, `id` can be considered a bit superfluous because its only purpose is to identify and distinguish between the players. The important thing is that the two players have a unique ID. The label attribute is what each player will print on the board, which just happens to be a unique value as well between both the players. Finally, the name attribute is used to print the name of each player in a human-readable way.

The /BoardServer.js class

This class abstracts a representation of the game of *Tic-tac-toe*, defining an interface where we can create and manage a game world with two players and a board.

```
var EventEmitter = require('events').EventEmitter;
var util = require('util');

/**
 *
 * @constructor
 */
var Board = function() {
    this.cells = [];
    this.players = [];
    this.currentTurn = 0;
    this.ready = false;

    this.init();
};

Board.events = {
    PLAYER_CONNECTED: 'playerConnected',
    GAME_READY: 'gameReady',
    CELL_MARKED: 'cellMarked',
    CHANGE_TURN: 'changeTurn',
    WINNER: 'winner',
    DRAW: 'draw'
};

util.inherits(Board, EventEmitter);
```

As this code is intended to run in the server only, it takes full advantage of Node.js. The first part of the script imports two core Node.js modules that we'll leverage instead of reinventing the wheel. The first, `EventEmitter`, will allow us to broadcast events about our game as they take place. Second, we import a utility class that lets us easily leverage object-oriented programming. Finally, we define some static variables related to the `Board` class in order to simplify event registration and propagation.

```
Board.prototype.mark = function(cellId) {
    // ...
    if (this.checkWinner()) {
         this.emit(Board.events.WINNER, {player:
this.players[this.currentTurn]});
    }
};
```

The `Board` class exposes several methods that a driver application can call in order to input data into it, and it emits events when certain situations occur. As illustrated in the method mentioned previously, whenever a player successfully marks an available square on the board, the game broadcasts that event so that the driver program knows what has happened in the game; it can then contact each client through their corresponding sockets, and let them know what happened.

The /server.js class

Here, we have the driver program that uses the `Board` class that we described previously in order to enforce the game's rules. It also uses WebSockets to maintain connected clients and handle their individual interaction with the game.

```
var WebSocketServer = require('ws').Server;
var Board = require('./BoardServer');
var Player = require('./Player');

var PORT = 2667;
var wss = new WebSocketServer({port: PORT});
var board = new Board();

var events = {
    incoming: {
        JOIN_GAME: 'csJoinGame',
        MARK: 'csMark',
        QUIT: 'csQuit'
    },
    outgoing: {
        JOIN_GAME: 'scJoinGame',
        MARK: 'scMark',
        SET_TURN: 'scSetTurn',
        OPPONENT_READY: 'scOpponentReady',
        GAME_OVER: 'scGameOver',
        ERROR: 'scError',
        QUIT: 'scQuit'
    }
};

/**
 *
 * @param action
 * @param data
 * @returns {*}
 */
```

```
function makeMessage(action, data) {
    var resp = {
        action: action,
        data: data
    };

    return JSON.stringify(resp);
}


console.log('Listening on port %d', PORT);
```

The first part of this Node.js server script imports both our custom classes (`Board` and `Player`) as well as a handy third-party library called `ws` that helps us implement the WebSocket server. This library handles things such as the setup of the initial connection, the protocol upgrade, and so on, since these steps are not included in the JavaScript WebSocket object, which is only intended to be used as a client. After a couple of convenience objects, we have a working server that waits for connections on `ws://localhost:2667`.

```
wss.on('connection', function connection(ws) {
    board.on(Board.events.PLAYER_CONNECTED, function(player) {
        wss.clients.forEach(function(client) {
            board.players.forEach(function(player) {
                client.send(makeMessage(events.outgoing.JOIN_GAME,
player));
            });
        });
    });

    ws.on('message', function incoming(msg) {
        try {
            var msg = JSON.parse(msg);
        } catch (error) {
            ws.send(makeMessage(events.outgoing.ERROR, 'Invalid
action'));
            return;
        }

        try {
            switch (msg.action) {
                case events.incoming.JOIN_GAME:
                    var player = new Player(board.players.length + 1,
board.players.length === 0 ? 'X' : 'O', msg.data);
                    board.addPlayer(player);
                    break;
```

```
            // ...
        }
    } catch (error) {
        ws.send(makeMessage(events.outgoing.ERROR, error.
message));
        }
    });
});
```

The rest of the important stuff with this server happens in the middle. For brevity, we've only included one example of each situation, which includes an event handler registration for events emitted by the Board class as well as registration of a callback function for events received by the socket. (Did you recognize the ws.on('message', function(msg){}) function call? This is Node's equivalent of the client-side JavaScript socket.onmessage = function(event){} that we discussed earlier.)

Of major importance here is the way we handle incoming messages from the game clients. Since the client can only send us a single string as the message, how are we to know what the message is? Since there are many types of messages that the client can send to the server, what we do here is create our own little protocol. That is, each message will be a serialized JSON object (also known as an object literal) with two attributes. The first will be keyed with the value of action and the second will have a key of data, which can have a different value depending on the specified action. From here, we can look at the value of msg.action and respond to it accordingly.

For example, whenever a client connects to the game server, it sends a message with the following value:

```
{
    action: events.outgoing.JOIN_GAME,
    data: "<player nickname>"
};
```

Once the server receives that object as the payload of the onmessage event, it can know what the message means and the expected value for the player's nickname.

The /public/js/Board.js class

This class is very similar to BoardServer.js, with the main difference being that it also handles the DOM (meaning the HTML elements rendered and managed by the browser), since the game needs to be rendered to human players.

```
/**
 *
 * @constructor
```

```
*/
var Board = function(scoreBoard) {
    this.cells = [];
    this.dom = document.createElement('table');
    this.dom.addEventListener('click', this.mark.bind(this));
    this.players = [];
    this.currentTurn = 0;
    this.ready = false;

    this.scoreBoard = scoreBoard;

    this.init();
};

Board.prototype.bindTo = function(container) {
    container.appendChild(this.dom);
};

Board.prototype.doWinner = function(pos) {
    this.disableAll();
    this.highlightCells(pos);
};
```

Again, for brevity, we have chosen not to display much of the game's logic. The important things to note here are that this version of the Board class is very much DOM-aware, and it behaves very passively to game decisions and the enforcement of the game's rules. Since we're using an authoritative server, this class does whatever the server tells it to, such as marking itself in a way that indicates that a certain participant has won the game.

The /public/js/app.js class

Similar to `server.js`, this script is the driver program for our game. It does two things: it takes input from the user with which it drives the server, and it uses input that it receives from the server in order to drive the board.

```
var socket = new WebSocket('ws://localhost:2667');

var scoreBoard = [
    document.querySelector('#p1Score'),
    document.querySelector('#p2Score')
];

var hero = {};
var board = new Board(scoreBoard);
```

```
board.onMark = function(cellId){
    socket.send(makeMessage(events.outgoing.MARK, {playerId: hero.id,
cellId: cellId}));
};

socket.onmessage = function(event){
    var msg = JSON.parse(event.data);

    switch (msg.action) {
        case events.incoming.GAME_OVER:
            if (msg.data.player) {
                board.doWinner(msg.data.pos);
            } else {
                board.doDraw();
            }

            socket.send(makeMessage(events.outgoing.QUIT, hero.id));
            break;

        case events.incoming.QUIT:
            socket.close();
            break;
    }
};

socket.onopen = function(event) {
    startBtn.removeAttribute('disabled');
    nameInput.removeAttribute('disabled');
    nameInput.removeAttribute('placeholder');
    nameInput.focus();
};
```

Again, it is noteworthy how DOM-centric the client server is. Observe also how obedient the client is to the messages received from the server. If the action specified by the server in the message that it sends to the clients is GAME_OVER, the client cleans things up, tells the player that the game is over either because someone won the game or the game ended in a draw, then it tells the server that it is ready to disconnect. Again, the client waits for the server to tell it what to do next. In this case, it waits for the server to clean up, then tells the client to disconnect itself.

Summary

In this chapter, we discussed the basics of networking and network programming paradigms. We saw how WebSockets makes it possible to develop real-time, multiplayer games in HTML5. Finally, we implemented a simple game client and game server using widely supported web technologies and built a fun game of *Tic-tac-toe*.

In the next chapter, we will take a look at the current state of the art in the JavaScript development world, including JavaScript in the server through Node.js. The chapter will teach you current techniques to manage the development cycle in JavaScript with workflow and resource management tools such as NPM, Bower, Grunt, and so on.

2
Setting Up the Environment

The goal of the last chapter was to introduce you to multiplayer game programming in JavaScript using current HTML5 technologies. Although we went over the implementation of a real multiplayer game, there was no mention made of how you might manage a more complex project.

Along with new technologies such as WebSockets, we can also attribute the great advance that has taken place within the web platform to the supporting tools that have been created to support project management and workflow of HTML5 and JavaScript development.

In this chapter, we will discuss the following principles and concepts:

- Developing JavaScript applications in **Node.js**
- Writing modular JavaScript applications
- Managing Node.js packages with **npm**
- Managing client-side packages with **Bower**
- Automating JavaScript development

JavaScript outside the browser with Node.js

It wasn't too many years ago when a so-called web developer used JavaScript on the rare occasion when a web form needed client-side validation. Since CSS wasn't as advanced as it is today, or at least it wasn't widely supported, JavaScript was also used in order to create image rollover effects. Not many years ago, the words JavaScript and programmer would not have gone well together.

However, times change and technologies evolve. Today, qualified JavaScript programmers are sought after and compensated very competitively relative to programmers of other programming languages. This is a reflection of how popular and powerful the JavaScript language has become.

As a result, JavaScript is steadily going from being *The World's Most Misunderstood Programming Language* (*Crockford, Douglas (2001).* `http://javascript.crockford.com/javascript.html`) to becoming an enterprise-level language, which is used in applications both inside the browser as well as in standalone programs, including server applications. As explained and illustrated in the last chapter, JavaScript is used in different ways when it is employed for the client-side build of your game as well as the game server.

You may remember that a game server doesn't have to be written in JavaScript. In fact, the game client has absolutely no idea what language the server is written in since all of its communication with the server takes place through the WebSocket protocol. However, since we want to maximize the amount of code that we can share between client and server, while reducing the overall amount of code that we write at the same time, we will write our games in a way where this sharing of code is possible. That is where Node.js comes into play.

Node.js

Without doubt, you've heard of Node.js by now. For those who are not exactly sure what Node actually is, it is simply a runtime environment built on Google Chrome's JavaScript engine (also known as **V8**). In other words, Node is neither a special version of JavaScript nor is it a standalone JavaScript engine, but rather, it is an entire ecosystem that happens to leverage Google's open source JavaScript engine, which happens to be, arguably, one of the seven wonders of the world today.

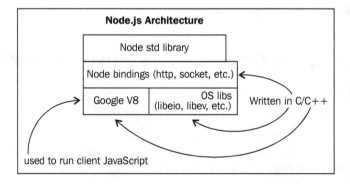

Two characteristics of Node.js that are worth mentioning are that Node.js is not tied to the browser, and every I/O operation is asynchronous.

As for it not being a browser environment, you will not find a window object like you do in a browser. In addition, since none of the restrictions that are imposed by a browser exist in the Node.js environment, you can take full advantage of the underlying operating system. First, think of whatever server-side language you have been using so far, or whatever programming language you were considering using to write your game servers that we discussed in *Chapter 1, Getting Started with Multiplayer Game Programming*. Then, replace that language in your mind with JavaScript. This is the big offer that Node.js makes.

Some of the benefits that you will find in using JavaScript on both ends of the stack (server side and client side) include the following:

- You can share a lot of the code that you write for the server and client
- You only need to master one language
- JavaScript is a powerful language that solves many of the problems that exist in other languages
- Since JavaScript is single threaded, you will never have deadlocks or many of the issues associated with multi-threaded programming

By now, I hope that you are able to see how fundamental Node.js can be in HTML5 multiplayer game development, or at least how crucial it will be in this book. Before we dive too deeply into some of the fundamental concepts, let us ensure that you can install and run it on your system.

Installing Node.js

The two recommended ways to install Node.js on your system are to download an executable file from the official website at `http://www.nodejs.org` or to install it manually by compiling the source code. Depending on your operating system of choice, you may also be able to install it via some package management system or a similar tool. Whatever method you decide to pursue, be sure to install the latest stable version, which, as of this writing, is Version 0.12.0.

Once you have installed Node.js on your system, you can take it for a test run by opening a terminal window and typing in the following commands:

```
node
console.log('Hello, World!');
```

If all goes well during the installation process, you should see an output similar to the one displayed in the following screenshot:

You can check the version of Node.js that you have installed by running the following command on your terminal:

```
node --version
```

Even though the latest version available today (as of this writing, in early 2015) is 0.12.0, all scripts described in this book are written in and tested against Version 0.10.25. For backward-and forward-compatibility issues and questions, be sure to reference Node.js's official backlogs.

Writing modular JavaScript

Before the advent of Node.js, given all of JavaScript's infamous restrictions, probably the biggest complaint that it received from developers was the lack of built-in support for a modular development process.

The best practice for modular JavaScript development was creating your components inside a literal object, which, in its own way, behaved somewhat like a namespace. The idea was to create an object in the global scope, then use the named properties inside that object to represent specific namespaces where you would declare your classes, functions, constants, and so on (or at least the JavaScript equivalent).

```
var packt = packt || {};
packt.math = packt.math || {};
packt.math.Vec2 = function Vec2(x, y) {
    // ...
};

var vec2d = new packt.math.Vec2(0, 1);
vec2d instanceof packt.math.Vec2; // true
```

In the previous code snippet, we create an empty object in case the `packt` variable doesn't exist. In case it does, we don't replace it with an empty object, but we assign a reference to it to the `packt` variable. We do the same with the math property, inside which we add a constructor function named `Vec2d`. Now, we can confidently create instances of that specific vector class, knowing that, if there is some other vector library in our global scope, even if it's also named `Vec2`, it won't clash with our version since our constructor function resides inside the `packt.math` object.

While this method worked relatively well for a long time, it does come with three drawbacks:

- Typing the entire namespace every time needs a lot of work
- Constantly referencing deeply nested functions and properties hurts performance
- Your code can easily be replaced by a careless assignment to a top-level `namespace` property

The good news is that today there is a better way to write modules in JavaScript. By recognizing the shortcomings of the old way of doing things, a few proposed standards have emerged to solve this very problem.

CommonJS

In 2009, the folks at Mozilla created a project that was aimed at defining a way to develop JavaScript applications that were freed from the browser. (refer to http:// en.wikipedia.org/wiki/CommonJS.) Two distinct features of this approach are the `require` statement, which is similar to what other languages offer, and the `exports` variable, from where all the code to be included on a subsequent call to the require function comes. Each exported module resides inside a separate file, making it possible to identify the file referenced by the `require` statement as well as isolate the code that makes up the module.

```
// - - - - - - - -
// player.js

var Player = function(x, y, width, height) {
    this.x = x;
    this.y = y;
    this.width = width;
    this.height = height;
};

Player.prototype.render = function(delta) {
    // ...
```

```
};

module.exports = Player;
```

This code creates a module inside a file named `player.js`. The takeaways here are as follows:

- The contents of your actual module are the same old, plain JavaScript that you're used to and are in love with
- Whatever code you wish to export is assigned to the `module.exports` variable

Before we look at how to make use of this module, let us expound on the last point mentioned previously. As a result of how JavaScript closures work, we can reference values in a file (within the file) that are not directly exported through `module.exports`, and the values cannot be accessed (or modified) outside the module.

```
// - - - - - - -
// player.js

// Not really a constant, but this object is invisible outside this
module/file
var defaults = {
    width: 16,
    height: 16
};

var Player = function(x, y, width, height) {
    this.x = x;
    this.y = y;
    this.width = width || defaults.width;
    this.height = height || defaults.height;
};

Player.prototype.render = function(delta) {
    // ...
};

module.exports = Player;
```

Note that the `Player` constructor function accepts a width and height value, which will be assigned to a local and corresponding width and height attribute on instances of that class. However, if we omit these values, instead of assigning undefined or null to the instance's attributes, we fallback to the values specified in the `defaults` object. The benefit is that the object cannot be accessed anywhere outside the module since we don't export the variable. Of course, if we make use of EcmaScript 6's `const` declaration, we could achieve read-only named constants, as well as through EcmaScript 5's `Object.defineProperty`, with the writable bit set to false. However, the point here still holds, which is that nothing outside an exported module has direct access to values within a module that were not exported through `module.exports`.

Now, to make use of CommonJs modules, we need to be sure that we can reach the code locally within the filesystem. In its simplest form, a require statement will look for a file (relative to the one provided) to include, where the name of the file matches the require statement.

```
// - - - - - - - -
// app.js

var Player = require('./player.js');
var hero = new Player(0, 0);
```

To run the script in the app.js file, we can use the following command within the same directory where `app.js` is stored:

```
node app.js
```

Assuming that the `app.js` and `player.js` files are stored in the same directory, Node should be able to find the file named `player.js`. If `player.js` was located in the parent directory from `app.js`, then the `require` statement would need to look like the following:

```
// - - - - - - - -
// test/player_test.js

var Player = require('./../player.js');
var hero = new Player(0, 0);
```

As you'll see later, we can use Node's package management system to import modules or entire libraries very easily. Doing so causes the imported packages to be stored in a methodical manner, which, as a result, makes requiring them into your code much easier.

The next way of requiring a module is by simply including the exported module's name in the require statement, as follows:

```
// - - - - - - -
// app.js

var Player = require('player.js');
var hero = new Player(0, 0);
```

If you run the previous file, you will see a fatal runtime error that looks something like the following screenshot:

```
rsilveira@carus: ~/formigone/html5multiplayer/ch2
File Edit View Search Terminal Help
rsilveira@carus:~/formigone/html5multiplayer/ch2$ node player_test.js

module.js:340
    throw err;
        ^
Error: Cannot find module 'player.js'
    at Function.Module._resolveFilename (module.js:338:15)
    at Function.Module._load (module.js:280:25)
    at Module.require (module.js:364:17)
    at require (module.js:380:17)
    at Object.<anonymous> (/home/rsilveira/formigone/html5multiplayer/ch2/player
_test.js:1:76)
    at Module._compile (module.js:456:26)
    at Object.Module._extensions..js (module.js:474:10)
    at Module.load (module.js:356:32)
    at Function.Module._load (module.js:312:12)
    at Function.Module.runMain (module.js:497:10)
rsilveira@carus:~/formigone/html5multiplayer/ch2$
```

The reason Node can't find the `player.js` file is because, when we don't specify the name of the file with a leading period (this means that the file included is relative to the current script), it will look for the file inside a directory named `node_modules` within the same directory as the current script.

If Node is unable to find a matching file inside `node_modules`, or if the current directory does not have a directory that is so named, it will look for a directory named `node_modules` along with a file with the same name, similar to the require statement in the parent directory of the current script. If the search there fails, it will go up one more directory level and look for the file inside a `node_modules` directory there. The search continues as far as the root of the filesystem.

Another way to organize your files into a reusable, self-contained module is to bundle your files in a directory within `node_modules` and make use of an `index.js` file that represents the entry point to the module.

```
// - - - - - - - -
// node_modules/MyPlayer/index.js

var Player = function(x, y, width, height) {
    this.x = x;
    this.y = y;
    this.width = width;
    this.height = height
};

module.exports = Player;

// - - - - - - - -
// player_test.js

var Player = require('MyPlayer');

var hero = new Player(0, 0);
console.log(hero);
```

Note that the name of the module, as specified in the `require` statement, now matches the name of a directory within `node_modules`. You can tell that Node will look for a directory instead of a filename that matches the one supplied in the `require` function when the name doesn't start with characters that indicate either a relative or absolute path ("/", "./", or "../") and the file extension is left out.

When Node looks for a directory name, as shown in the preceding example, it will first look for an `index.js` file within the matched directory and return its contents. If Node doesn't find an `index.js` file, it will look for a file named `package.json`, which is a manifest file that describes the module.

```
// - - - - - - - -
// node_modules/MyPlayer/package.json

{
    "name": "MyPlayer",
    "main": "player.js"
}
```

Assuming that we have renamed the `node_modules/MyPlayer/index.js` file as `node_modules/MyPlayer/player.js`, all will work as before.

Later in this chapter, when we talk about npm, we will dive deeper into `package.json` since it plays an important role in the Node.js ecosystem.

RequireJS

An alternative project that attempts to solve JavaScript's lack of native script importing and a standard module specification is RequireJS. (refer to `http://requirejs.org/`.) Actually, RequireJS is a specific implementation of the **Asynchronous Module Definition (AMD)** specification. AMD is a specification that defines an API for *defining modules such that the module and its dependencies can be asynchronously loaded* [Burke, James (2011). `https://github.com/amdjs/amdjs-api/wiki/AMD`].

A distinctive difference between CommonJS and RequireJS is that RequireJS is designed for use inside a browser, whereas CommonJS doesn't have a browser in mind. However, both methods can be adapted for the browser (in the case of CommonJS) as well as for other environments (in the case of RequireJS).

Similar to CommonJS, RequireJS can be thought of as having two parts: a module definition script and a second script that consumes (or requires) the modules. In addition, similar to CommonJS but more obvious in RequireJS, is the fact that every app has a single entry point. This is where the requiring begins.

```
// - - - - - - - -
// index.html

<script data-main="scripts/app" src="scripts/require.js"></script>
```

Here, we include the `require.js` library in an HTML file, specifying the entry point, which is indicated by the `data-main` attribute. Once the library loads, it will attempt to load a script named `app.js` that is located in a directory named `scripts`, which is stored on the same path as the host `index.html` file.

Two things to note here are that the `scripts/app.js` script is loaded asynchronously, as opposed to the default way all scripts are loaded by the browser when using a `script` tag. Furthermore, `scripts/app.js` can itself require other scripts, which will in turn be loaded asynchronously.

By convention, the entry point script (`scripts/app.js` in the previous example) will load a configuration object so that RequireJS can be adapted to your own environment and then the real application entry point is loaded.

```
// - - - - - - -
// scripts/app.js

requirejs.config({
    baseUrl: 'scripts/lib',
    paths: {
        app: '../app'
    }
});

requirejs(['jquery', 'app/player'], function ($, player) {
    // ...
});
```

In the previous example, we first configure the script loader, then we require two modules—first the jQuery library and then a module named `player`. The `baseUrl` option in the configuration block tells RequireJS to load all the scripts from the `scripts/lib` directory, which is relative to the file that loaded `scripts/app.js` (in this case, `index.html`). The path's attribute allows you to create exceptions to that `baseUrl`, rewriting the path to scripts whose require name (known as the **module ID**) starts with, in this case, the `app` string . When we require `app/player`, RequireJS will load a script, which is relative to `index.html`, `scripts/app/player.js`.

Once those two modules are loaded, RequireJS will invoke the callback function that you passed to the `requirejs` function, adding the modules that were requested as parameters in the same order as specified.

You may be wondering why we talked about both CommonJS and RequireJS since the goal is to share as much code as possible between the server and the client. The reason for covering both methods and tools is for completeness and information purposes only. Since Node.js already uses CommonJS for its module-loading strategy, there is little reason to use RequireJS in the server. Instead of mixing RequireJS for use in the browser, what is commonly done (this will be the approach of choice for the rest of the book) is to use CommonJS for everything (including **client-side** code) and then run a tool called **Browserify** over the client code, making it possible to load scripts in the browser that make use of CommonJS. We'll cover Browserify shortly.

Managing Node.js packages with Npm

Npm is a package manager for JavaScript and is similar to **Composer** for PHP or **Pip** for Python. (go to https://www.npmjs.com/.) Some people may assure you that npm stands for Node Package Manager, but although it has been Node.js's default package manager since version 0.6.3, npm is not an acronym. Thus, you will often see npm spelled in lowercase.

To quickly check if you have npm installed, you can use a terminal window to query the version of npm that you have installed.

```
npm -v
```

For instructions on how to install npm on your particular operating system, ensure that you follow the guidelines on npm's official website. The version used in the sample codes and demo applications in this book is version 1.3.10.

When using npm to install third-party packages, you can choose to install them either locally for your project, or globally so that the package will be visible anywhere in your system.

```
npm install watch
```

By default, when you install a package (in the previous example, we install a package named watch that watches directories and files for changes) with no flags, the package is installed locally (assuming a package.json file also exists) and saved to a node_modules directory relative to where the command was executed.

To install a package globally or system-wide, just append the -g flag to the install command:

```
npm install watch -g
```

By convention, if you need a package that is used within your code through require statements, you will want to save the package locally. If the intent is to use the package as an executable code from your command line, then you will normally want to install it globally.

If you want to build on your package.json manifest so that the local packages your project depends on can be shared and easily installed, you can either edit the manifest file manually, adding the dependency to the json object under the "dependencies" key, or you can let npm do that for you, but without forgetting to specify the --save flag:

```
npm install watch --save
```

Note that running the previous command will download the code that makes up the requested package into your working directory as well as update your `package.json` manifest so that you can later update the packages or install them anew, as needed. In other words, you can always use your existing `package.json` file to rebuild your development environment as far as your third-party dependencies are concerned.

Once you have one or more dependencies specified in your `package.json` file, you can install them by running npm, as follows:

```
npm install
```

This will download all the dependencies in your manifest file and save them into `node_modules`.

Similarly, you can update packages through npm by using the update command:

```
npm update
```

If you don't know how to get started to create a `package.json` manifest file, you can let npm help you to fill in the blanks for the most common attributes.

```
npm init
```

This will load an interactive utility that asks you to enter values for the various attributes for the manifest, such as the package name, version, author name, and so on. It also offers some same default values so that you can either ignore attributes you don't know what they do, or you can trust npm with whatever fallback option it offers you, making it easy for you to quickly get a manifest file going.

```
npm init
// … assume all proposed default values

// - - - - - - - -
// package.json

{
  "name": "npm",
  "version": "0.0.0",
  "description": "ERROR: No README data found!",
  "main": "index.js",
  "scripts": {
    "test": "echo \"Error: no test specified\" && exit 1"
  },
  "author": "",
  "license": "BSD-2-Clause"
}
```

Once you have a generic `package.json` manifest, you can add your dependencies to it with npm install commands.

```
npm install browserify --save

// - - - - - - -
// package.json

{
    "name": "npm",
    "version": "0.0.0",
    "description": "ERROR: No README data found!",
    "main": "index.js",
    "scripts": {
        "test": "echo \"Error: no test specified\" && exit 1"
    },
    "author": "",
    "license": "BSD-2-Clause" ,
    "dependencies": {
        "browserify": "~9.0.3"
    }
}
```

Of course, you can always edit the file manually to change values or remove attributes that you feel are unnecessary, such as license, description, or version. Some attributes are only meaningful if you plan to share your package privately or with the global npm registry. Other values, such as scripts, are used for convenience during development. For example, we can register a script to be executed when we run npm `<script value>`.

```
// - - - - - - -
// package.json

{
  "scripts": {
      "test": "node test.js"
    }
}

// - - - - - - -
// test.js

console.log('testing npm scripts');
```

Thus, we can have Node run a script named `test.js` through npm with the following command:

```
npm test
```

While you may not be saving a lot of typing by using npm in this case, you do make it more standard for others to know, for example, how to run your tests, even if your test runner scripts are not named or executed in any particular standard form.

Managing frontend packages with Bower

If you're not impressed enough with npm as a backend JavaScript package manager, perhaps Bower will take you to the next level of joy. (Refer to `http://bower.io/`.) Bower works very similarly to npm. In fact, most commands and conventions that we've just discussed for npm work verbatim in Bower.

In fact, Bower itself is a Node.js module that is installed through npm:

```
npm install bower -g
```

We can interact with Bower the same way we've interacted with npm so far.

```
bower init
// … using all proposed defaults

// - - - - - - - -
// bower.json

{
  name: 'npm',
  version: '0.0.0',
  homepage: 'https://github.com/formigone',
  authors: [
    'Rodrigo Silveira <webmaster@rodrigo-silveira.com>'
  ],
  license: 'MIT',
  ignore: [
    '**/.*',
    'node_modules',
    'bower_components',
    'test',
    'tests'
  ]
}
```

Bower makes use of a `bower.json` manifest file, which by now should look somewhat familiar to you. To install dependencies, either edit the manifest by hand or leverage Bower.

```
bower install jquery -save

// - - - - - - -
// bower.json

{
  name: 'npm',
  version: '0.0.0',
  homepage: 'https://github.com/formigone',
  authors: [
    'Rodrigo Silveira <webmaster@rodrigo-silveira.com>'
  ],
  license: 'MIT',
  ignore: [
    '**/.*',
    'node_modules',
    'bower_components',
    'test',
    'tests'
  ],
  "dependencies": {
    "jquery": "~2.1.3"
  }
}
```

The main difference between Bower and npm, as should be apparent by now, is that Bower deals with frontend dependencies, which can be JavaScript, CSS, HTML, font files, and so on. Bower will save dependencies inside a `bower_components` directory, similar to npm's `node_dependencies`.

Browserify

Finally, let us use this very handy npm package to leverage our CommonJS modules (as well as Node's native modules) for use in the browser. This is exactly what Browserify does: it takes an entry point script, follows all require statements recursively from that file down, then inlines all files in the dependency tree that it builds, and returns a single file. (Refer to `http://browserify.org/`.) This way, when a browser runs across a require statement in one of your scripts, it doesn't have to fetch the file from the filesystem; it fetches the file from within the same file.

```
sudo npm install browserify -g
```

Once we have installed Browserify (again, since this is intended to be used as a command line tool, we install it globally), we can `bundle` all of our CommonJS files in one.

```
// - - - - - - - -
// app.js

var Player = require('MyPlayer');

var hero = new Player(0, 0);
console.log(hero);

// - - - - - - - -
// node_modules/MyPlayer/index.js

var defaults = {
    width: 16,
    height: 16
};

var Player = function(x, y, width, height) {
    this.x = x;
    this.y = y;
    this.width = width || defaults.width;
    this.height = height || defaults.height;
};

Player.prototype.render = function(delta) {
    // ...
};

module.exports = Player;
```

Browserify will take care of requiring all of the dependencies as needed so that the output file will have all of its dependencies ready to be used, as shown in the preceding code sample.

Browserify takes the name of the entry point as the first argument and prints the output to standard output by default. Alternately, we can specify a filename where the bundle will be saved.

```
browserify app.js -o bundle.js
```

Browserify will now create a file named `bundle.js`, which we can include in an HTML file and use in the browser. Additionally, we can compress the output file with any of the many available tools that are found in npm's registry.

```
sudo npm install uglify-js -g
uglifyjs bundle.js -o bundle.min.js --source-map bundle.min.js.map
```

Running the preceding code will install a node package named **UglifyJS**, which parses, mangles, compresses, and shrink-wraps our `bundle.js` file very smartly. (Refer to `https://github.com/mishoo/UglifyJS`.) The output will be both very small in size and not at all readable by humans. As a bonus, it creates a `source map` file, which allows us to debug the minified file by mapping it back to the original `bundle.js` file in its original form.

Automating your workflow

So far, we have learned how to perform the following tasks:

- Writing modular JavaScript code that can be imported into other modules
- Reusing modules in client and server code through CommonJS and Browserify
- Managing node packages with npm
- Managing client packages with Bower

Now we're ready to bring this all together in a way that takes the burden of running all these commands away from us. Picture for a moment what it would be like if you had to write a few lines of code, save your work, skip over to the command line, run Browserify, then run Uglify-js, then run your unit tests, followed by a handful of other npm tools, and then finally hop over to a browser, refresh the browser, and see the updated app working. Oh, wait! You forgot to restart the game server, which is a Node.js app, and needs to be restarted after you change those files. So, you go back to the terminal, run a few more commands, and eventually, you see the new code in the browser.

If that mental exercise just made all those wonderful tools that we covered earlier in the chapter look like a lot of work, remain calm. There is yet another set of tools that we can count on to make our lives easier, and JavaScript development is a thing of beauty (as opposed to what it is commonly called, particularly by those who do not use the tools that we'll now discuss).

Grunt

Grunt is a popular task runner tool that automates repetitive tasks you may need to do, such as running unit tests, bundling components, minifying bundles, creating API documentation from your source file comments, and so on. (Refer to `http://gruntjs.com/`.)

Grunt uses the concept of plugins, which are specific task configurations that can be shared and reused. For example, it is likely that you will want a plugin that watches a directory for changes, then runs Browserify when a change is triggered. (In other words, every time you save a file, a task will be run.)

You can write your own plugins by hand; although this is a straightforward process, it is verbose enough, so we will not get into it in this book. Thankfully, Grunt has a vast plugin listing with a plugin for just about everything that you will ever need, or at least everything that we will need for the purpose of this book.

```
npm install grunt-cli -g
```

No surprise here! We install Grunt through npm. Next, we need to install Grunt plugins using npm and `package.json`; the only thing is that we list them under `devDependencies` and not dependencies.

```
npm install grunt --save-dev
npm install grunt-browserify --save-dev
npm install grunt-contrib-watch --save-dev
npm install grunt-contrib-uglify --save-dev
```

Next, we create a `Gruntfile.js` to configure our tasks. This file specifies *targets* and defines the behavior of each target. Most of the time, you will simply look at sample configuration files for whatever plugin you use and then tweak it to fit your needs.

In the specific case of using watch and Browserify, we need to simply tell the watch plugin to run the Browserify task when a change is observed, and in the Browserify task, we need to specify the most basic settings: an entry point file and an output bundle file.

The four parts that make up the `Gruntfile` are as follows:

- A boilerplate wrapper function
- The configuration for each task
- Manual loading of each plugin that is used by the task
- Registration of each task so that Grunt can execute them

```
// - - - - - - - -
// Gruntfile.js
```

```
module.exports = function(grunt) {

    grunt.initConfig({
        browserify: {
            client: {
                src: ['./app.js'],
                dest: 'bundle.js'
            }
        },
        watch: {
            files: ['**/*'],
            tasks: ['browserify'],
        }
    });

    grunt.loadNpmTasks('grunt-browserify');
    grunt.loadNpmTasks('grunt-contrib-watch');

    grunt.registerTask('default', ['watch']);

};
```

Inside `grunt.initConfig`, you configure each task, with the attribute name matching the name of the task. You then load each plugin calling the `loadNpmTasks` function and loading the corresponding dependency. Finally, you specify default tasks as well as any custom tasks and map them to their dependencies. Using the name used in the task registration will run that particular task.

```
grunt browserify
```

The preceding command will run the browserify task, which has been configured and loaded as shown previously. If you run the grunt command with no task specified will run the `default` task, which, in this case, will run the watch task.

Gulp

Gulp is a popular alternative to Grunt, which claims to improve on Grunt by offering simpler configuration. (Refer to `http://gulpjs.com/`.) Whichever tool you use is up to you. Much like the kind of car you drive or the fast food restaurant you visit, using Gulp or Grunt is all about taste and personal preference.

```
npm install gulp -g
npm install gulp-uglify --save-dev
npm install gulp --save-dev
```

Gulp uses `gulpfile.js` as its configuration file.

```
// - - - - - - -
// gulpfile.js

var gulp = require('gulp');
var uglify = require('gulp-uglify');

gulp.task('minify', function () {
    gulp.src('app.js')
        .pipe(uglify())
        .pipe(gulp.dest('build'))
});
```

The preceding configuration should look much more straightforward as compared to Grunt. If looking at it you guess that a task named minify is registered, taking a source file called `app.js` that is first uglified, then saved to a build directory, you guessed right.

To run the task, you can specify a default task or explicitly run the previously mentioned one with the following command:

```
gulp minify
```

Summary

In this chapter, we covered a lot of ground, explaining the opportunity we have with Node.js bringing JavaScript to the server. We saw ways to build manageable modules in JavaScript, share and reuse these modules on both ends of the stack, and use management and workflow tools, such as npm, Bower, Grunt, and Gulp, to automate the development process.

Now, we are ready to take full advantage of the Node.js ecosystem along with the powerful supporting workflow tools that are available. From here, we will get back to writing games by building a fun multiplayer snake game. We will discuss concepts that will allow us to match players together in the same game world, which is a fundamental part of bringing players into your game.

3
Feeding a Snake in Real Time

After having covered the introductory material until now, it is time to let the rubber hit the road. This chapter will walk you through the upgrade of a single-player game into its multiplayer counterpart.

Unlike the game we developed in *Chapter 1, Getting Started with Multiplayer Game Programming*, this game will need to be played in real-time, as opposed to being turn-based, which brings a whole set of challenges to the table. Once we solve the fundamental problems associated with synchronizing real-time game worlds across two or more players, we'll look into other fundamental, yet more involving concepts.

In this chapter, we will discuss the following principles and concepts:

- Fixing your game loop for multiplayer gaming
- Implementing an authoritative server
- The lobby and room system
- Matchmaking algorithms
- Socket programming with **Socket.io**

Hello world for game development

Surely, you must have written a *hello world* program when you were learning programming. In game development, I'd say the classic *hello world* game every developer should start with is snake. The concept is simple: move a block around the screen collecting special blocks that cause your block to stretch into a sequence of connected blocks that resemble the movement of a snake. If you run the head of the snake into its body, you lose.

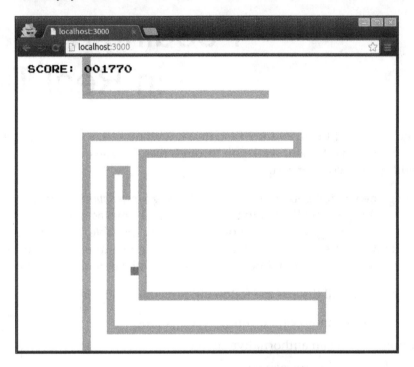

This implementation only allows the snake to move up, down, left, or right. Once you specify the direction for the snake to move, it will continue moving in that direction until you move it in a different direction. As a bonus, this particular implementation allows you to wrap around the screen—that is, if you move outside one of the sides of the screen, the snake will appear on the opposite side.

Catching a red block makes the snake grow by one extra block and increments your score by 10 points. Running the snake into itself stops the game loop and prints a simple game over message.

In order to keep things simple for this initial version, there aren't any additional screens, including a main entry screen. The game simply begins once it is fully loaded. As we build upon this single player version of the game, we'll add the required screens that will make it more intuitive and user friendly for more than one player to join the game.

Setting up the game

The goal of this initial single player version of the game is to make a playable game with as few lines of code by using the most basic model that we can build on. Thus, many additional details are left as an exercise for you.

In preparation for the next step, where we'll add server-side components to the game, we've written the first version of the game using Node.js and exported it to the browser using Browserify, as discussed in *Chapter 2, Setting Up the Environment*.

package.json

In keeping with the theme of making everything as simple possible, we will use a package.json file that only requires the **Express** framework to help us with routing and the Grunt plugins to help us to automatically build and export our modules with Browserify:

```
// ch3/package.json
{
    "name": "snake-ch3",
    "dependencies": {
        "express": "*",
        "express-generator": "*"
    },
    "devDependencies": {
        "grunt": "~0.4.5",
        "grunt-browserify": "~3.4.0",
        "grunt-contrib-uglify": "~0.8.0",
        "grunt-contrib-watch": "~0.6.1"
    }
}
```

Express.js is a web framework for Node.js that allows us to very quickly set up the entire web server to host and serve our game. (refer to http://expressjs.com/.) While Express plays a major role in our project, as it routes user requests for the appropriate files, understanding how it works is not a prerequisite to this chapter or the rest of the book. We will cover enough of the absolute basics to get you started using this powerful framework.

With all this in place, we use the Express command-line tool to build the project.

```
npm install
express snake-ch3
cd snake-ch3
npm install
```

After executing the preceding sequence of commands, we have set up our boilerplate Node.js server with all of Express' defaults, which, for our purpose, will work just fine. If anything goes wrong for whatever reason, there will be enough error messages to help you understand why and what the problems are. Provided that everything seems to be going fine after you enter the preceding commands, you can now test the project by starting your server with the following command:

```
npm start
```

This will start the server on port 3000, which you can load on your modern browser of choice at http://localhost:3000/.

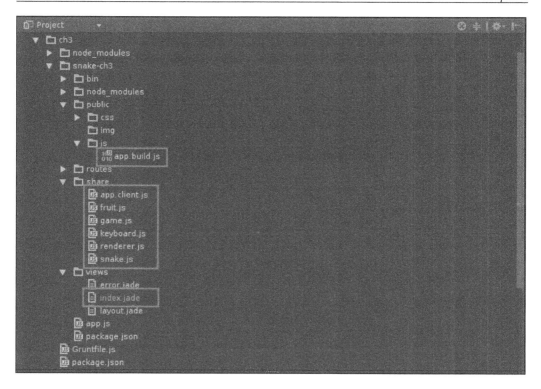

The project structure will now look like the one in the preceding screenshot, except for the files enclosed within the red box that will not be generated by Express Generator. We will be creating and editing these files by hand, as you will see in the next several sections.

Index.jade

By default, Express will create an index file that displays a welcome message. Since all we need for now is a single screen to display the game, we'll just edit this file for our own purpose:

```
// ch3/snake-ch3/views/index.jade
extends layout

block content
  div#gameArea
    p#scoreA SCORE: <span>000000</span>
    p#gameOver.animated.pulse.hidden Game Over
    canvas#gameCanvas
    div#statsPanel
  script(src='/js/app.build.js')
```

If you squint hard enough, you will see the HTML markup. If you're not familiar with the Jade templating language that Express uses by default, don't worry. What we do in the template is create a `<p>` element where we'll display the current score, one for the game over message, and a canvas element that we'll use to render the game. We also include the main script file, which is the output of the Grunt task that concatenates all our files and runs Browserify over them so that we can load it in the browser. Since `index.jade` is the only thing we'll see of Jade in this book, we won't go into it any further. For more information about how Jade works and what it can do, visit its website at `http://www.jade-lang.com`.

The game modules

With the preceding structure in place, all that we need now is a couple of classes that implement the game. We'll do this in five classes so that we can reuse individual pieces of logic when we implement the game server.

Game.js

Here's how we'll implement our `game.js` file:

```
// ch3/snake-ch3/share/game.js
var Game = function (fps) {
    this.fps = fps;
    this.delay = 1000 / this.fps;
    this.lastTime = 0;
    this.raf = 0;

    this.onUpdate = function (delta) {
    };
    this.onRender = function () {
    };
};

Game.prototype.update = function (delta) {
    this.onUpdate(delta);
};

Game.prototype.render = function () {
    this.onRender();
};

Game.prototype.loop = function (now) {
    this.raf = requestAnimationFrame(this.loop.bind(this));
```

```
        var delta = now - this.lastTime;
        if (delta >= this.delay) {
            this.update(delta);
            this.render();
            this.lastTime = now;
        }
    };

    Game.prototype.start = function () {
        if (this.raf < 1) {
            this.loop(0);
        }
    };

    Game.prototype.stop = function () {
        if (this.raf > 0) {
            cancelAnimationFrame(this.raf);
            this.raf = 0;
        }
    };

    module.exports = Game;
```

This module is the cornerstone of our project. It defines a very simple interface that abstracts away a simple game loop. All that we need to do when we implement this class is define the update() and render() methods.

You will notice the use of requestAnimationFrame, which is a special function defined by browsers to help us render the game. Since the game server won't render the game, neither will it have the function available to it, we'll need to adapt to that when we start working on the server. We'll talk more about frame rate independence in the next section.

snake.js

We'll be adding the following code to our snake.js file:

```
// ch3/snake-ch3/share/snake.js
var keys = require('./keyboard.js');
var EventEmitter = require('events').EventEmitter;
var util = require('util');

var Snake = function (id, x, y, color_hex, width, height) {
    this.id = id;
```

```
        this.color = color_hex;
        this.head = {x: x, y: y};
        this.pieces = [this.head];
        this.width = width || 16;
        this.height = height || 16;
        this.readyToGrow = false;
        this.input = {};
    };

    Snake.events = {
        POWER_UP: 'Snake:powerup',
        COLLISION: 'Snake:collision'
    };

    util.inherits(Snake, EventEmitter);

    Snake.prototype.setKey = function (key) {
        this.input[keys.UP] = false;
        this.input[keys.DOWN] = false;
        this.input[keys.LEFT] = false;
        this.input[keys.RIGHT] = false;
        this.input[key] = true;
    };

    Snake.prototype.update = function (delta) {
        if (this.readyToGrow) {
            this.pieces.push({x: -10, y: -10});
            this.readyToGrow = false;
        }

        for (var len = this.pieces.length, i = len - 1; i > 0; i--) {
            this.pieces[i].x = this.pieces[i - 1].x;
            this.pieces[i].y = this.pieces[i - 1].y;
        }

        if (this.input[keys.LEFT]) {
            this.head.x += -1;
        } else if (this.input[keys.RIGHT]) {
            this.head.x += 1;
        } else if (this.input[keys.UP]) {
            this.head.y += -1;
        } else if (this.input[keys.DOWN]) {
            this.head.y += 1;
        }
```

```
};

Snake.prototype.checkCollision = function(){
    var collide = this.pieces.some(function(piece, i){
        return i > 0 && piece.x === this.head.x && piece.y === this.
head.y;
    }, this);

    if (collide) {
        this.emit(Snake.events.COLLISION, {id: this.id, point: this.
head, timestamp: performance.now()});
    }
};

Snake.prototype.grow = function() {
    this.readyToGrow = true;
    this.emit(Snake.events.POWER_UP, {id: this.id, size: this.pieces.
length, timestamp: performance.now()});
};

module.exports = Snake;
```

The snake class extends Node's EventEmitter class so that it can emit events to the main application. This way we can isolate the specific behavior of the class and decouple it from any concrete implementation that responds to the snake as per our choice.

We also create a simple interface that the main application can use to control the snake. Again, since the immediate goal of this version is to get the game running in a browser, we will make use of browser-specific functionality, which in this case is window.performance.now(), which we'll replace with a module compatible with Node.js when we need to.

Other supporting modules

There are three other classes (namely, fruit.js, keyboard.js, and renderer.js) that merely wrap the canvas and canvas context objects, a JavaScript equivalent of an enumeration to help us refer to keyboard input, and a simple point that we'll use to represent the pellet that the snake will eat. For brevity, we will omit the code for these classes.

app.client.js

Here's how our `app.client.js` module should look like:

```
// ch3/snake-ch3/share/app.client.js
game.onUpdate = function (delta) {
    var now = performance.now();

    // Check if there's no fruits left to be eaten. If so, create a
new one.
    if (fruits.length < 1) {
        fruitDelta = now - lastFruit;

        // If there's been enough time without a fruit for the snakes,
        // create a new one at a random position, and place it in the
world
        if (fruitDelta >= fruitDelay) {
            fruits[0] = new Fruit(
                parseInt(Math.random() * renderer.canvas.width / BLOCK_
WIDTH / 2, 10),
                parseInt(Math.random() * renderer.canvas.width / BLOCK_
HEIGHT / 2, 10),
                '#c00', BLOCK_WIDTH, BLOCK_HEIGHT
            );
        }
    }

    player.update(delta);
    player.checkCollision();

    // Check if the snake has gone outside the game board.
    // If so, wrap it around to the other side
    if (player.head.x < 0) {
        player.head.x = parseInt(renderer.canvas.width / player.width,
10);
    }

    if (player.head.x > parseInt(renderer.canvas.width / player.width,
10)) {
        player.head.x = 0;
    }

    if (player.head.y < 0) {
        player.head.y = parseInt(renderer.canvas.height / player.
height, 10);
    }
```

```
    if (player.head.y > parseInt(renderer.canvas.height / player.
height, 10)) {
        player.head.y = 0;
    }

    // Check if there's a fruit to be eaten. If so, check if the snake
has just
    // eaten it. If so, grow the player that ate it.
    if (fruits.length > 0) {
        if (player.head.x === fruits[0].x && player.head.y ===
fruits[0].y) {
            fruits = [];
            player.grow();
            lastFruit = now;
        }
    }
};

game.onRender = function () {
    ctx.clearRect(0, 0, renderer.canvas.width, renderer.canvas.
height);

    ctx.fillStyle = player.color;
    player.pieces.forEach(function(piece){
        ctx.fillRect(
            piece.x * player.width,
            piece.y * player.height,
            player.width,
            player.height
        );
    });

    fruits.forEach(function(fruit){
        ctx.fillStyle = fruit.color;
        ctx.fillRect(
            fruit.x * fruit.width,
            fruit.y * fruit.height,
            fruit.width,
            fruit.height
        );
    });
};
```

The first part of the app.client module, which is the concrete implementation of the game, imports all the required classes and modules and instantiates the game loop and player classes. Next (as seen previously) we implement the two game loop life cycle methods, namely the update and render methods. The only change that we'll need to make to these two methods when we add multiplayer functionality is to update and render an array of snakes rather than a single one.

Since the actual update for each player is delegated to the snake class itself, the game loop has no issues over what is done inside that method. In fact, the game loop doesn't even care about the output of the update methods, as we'll see later. The key here is that the game loop's update method allows every entity in the game to update itself during the update phase.

Similarly, during the render phase, the game loop only cares about rendering the current state of each entity that it wants to render. Although we could have also delegated the rendering of the snake and other visual entities, we'll leave the concrete rendering inside the game loop for simplicity.

Finally, at the end of the app.client module, we hook up to the incoming events that we care about. Here, we listen for game events that were created by the snake object. The Snake.events.POWER_UP and Snake.events.COLLISION custom events let us execute callback functions to respond to when the snake consumes a pellet and collides with itself respectively.

Next, we bind to the keyboard and listen for key press events. Due to the game mechanics that we implement, we don't care about any keys that are not being pressed, so that's why we don't register any listeners for these events. This particular block of code is a great candidate for refactoring later on since the way the client will receive this kind of input will be different from the server. For example, the client will still take input directly from the user using the same keyboard events as input, but the server will receive this input from the user, which will notify the server of its state through the socket connection:

```
// whenever we receive a POWER_UP event from the game, we
// update the player's score and display its value inside scoreWidget.
player.on(Snake.events.POWER_UP, function(event){
    var score = event.size * 10;
    scoreWidgets.filter(function( widget){
        return widget.id === event.id;
    })
        .pop()
        .el.textContent = '000000'.slice(0, - (score + '').length) +
score + '';
});
```

```
// whenever we receive a COLLISION event from the game, we
// stop the game and display a game over message to the player.
player.on(Snake.events.COLLISION, function(event){
    scoreWidgets.filter(function(widget){
        return widget.id === event.id;
    })
        .pop()
        .el.parentElement.classList.add('gameOver');

    game.stop();
    setTimeout(function(){
        ctx.fillStyle = '#f00';
        ctx.fillRect(event.point.x * player.width, event.point.y *
player.height, player.width, player.height);
    }, 0);

    setTimeout(function(){
        gameOver.classList.remove('hidden');
    }, 100);
});

document.body.addEventListener('keydown', function (e) {
    var key = e.keyCode;

    switch (key) {
        case keys.ESC:
            game.stop();
            break;
        case keys.SPACEBAR:
            game.start();
            break;
        case keys.LEFT:
        case keys.RIGHT:
        case keys.UP:
        case keys.DOWN:
            player.setKey(key);
            break;
        case keys.D:
            console.log(player.pieces);
            break;
    }
});
```

The game loop

As you know, the game loop is the very core of any real-time game. Although the game loop serves a fairly simple function, let us now consider some of the implications of having a game server and client running together.

Frame rate independence

The purpose of the game loop is nothing more than to ensure that the game runs in a consistent, ordered manner. For example, if we draw the current game state before we update it, the player might find the game to be slightly out of sync when they interact with it since the current display would be at least one frame behind what the player would expect it to be.

In addition, and this is particularly so in JavaScript's event-based input system, if we update the game every time we receive input from the user, we might have different parts of the game updating at different times, making the experience even more out of sync.

Thus, we put a game loop in place to ensure that, after any input is handled and cached and until the next `tick` of the game loop, we can apply the input during the `update` phase of the game step and then render the outcome of the update:

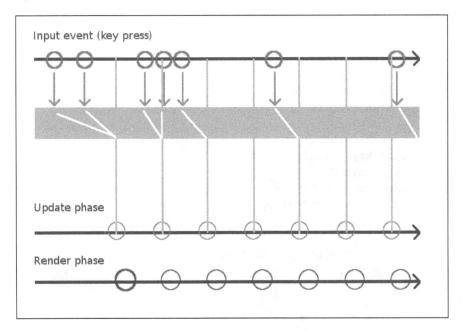

The most obvious solution to this problem is to model the input space within your game; then, query this during the `update` phase and respond accordingly. In other programming environments, we can simply query the input devices directly. Since JavaScript exposes events instead, we can't ask the runtime whether the left key is currently pressed.

Next, we need to update the game, which in most cases means that we'll move something just a tiny bit. After a few frames have been updated, these small movements that we've updated in each iteration will combine to create a smooth motion. In practical terms, what we need to do once the game loop has completed a cycle is to call the game loop again for the next cycle:

```
while (true) {
    update();
    render();
}
```

While a traditional game loop in most other programming languages might look something like the preceding code snippet, we can't do this in JavaScript because the while loop would block JavaScript's single thread, causing the browser to lock up:

```
function tick() {
    setTimeout(tick, 0.016);
    update();
    render();
}
```

A more appropriate approach in JavaScript is to use one of the timer functions (either `setTimeout` or `setInterval`) to call the game step method. While this solution actually works, unlike the while loop idea, we can run into issues such as the game consuming too much CPU (as well as the battery life of a mobile device), particularly when the loop continues to execute when the game is not running. We can also run into issues with the timer approach if JavaScript is busy with other things, and the `tick` function can't be called as often as we'd like.

You may wonder why we make the call to setTimeout and requestAnimationFrame at the beginning of the tick method, instead of at the end, after we have actually executed the code inside the method.

The reason for this is that calling either of these two functions simply schedules the callback function to run at the next event loop cycle. Calling setTimeout or requestAnimationFrame returns execution to the next command in the function calling it immediately, then the rest of the function executes to completion.

Once the function returns, JavaScript will execute the next piece of code in the event loop, which was added to the loop some time in the past. In other words, if JavaScript detects user input while we're executing our game tick method or some other event takes place, these events will be added to the queue and will be handled after our tick method returns. Thus, if we wait until the end of the tick method to schedule it again with the event loop, we may find the tick method waiting in line (so that it can have a turn at the CPU again) before other callbacks are handled.

By scheduling the tick method early on, we can be sure that it will be called again as soon as it can after it completes its current execution, even if other events are triggered during the current execution, and other code is placed on the event loop.

Finally, the most appropriate way to write a game loop in JavaScript is to use the more recent window.requireAnimationFrame function:

```
function tick(timestamp) {
    var rafId = requestAnimationFrame(tick);
    update();
    render();
}
```

RequestAnimationFrame is a handy function implemented in browsers that we can use to ask the browser to invoke our callback function right before the browser performs its next repaint. Since the inner workings of the browser are outside the scope of JavaScript, the refreshing rate is now at the operating system level, which is much more precise. In addition, since the browser knows when it needs to repaint and is much closer to the display device than JavaScript can possibly be, it can make many optimizations that we couldn't do on our own.

Calling requestAnimationFrame will return an integer value that will map to the provided function in the callback list. We can use this ID number to cancel our callback from being triggered when the browser determines that it should have. This is a handy way to pause execution of the game loop without using a conditional statement at the beginning of the callback, which would normally evaluate to false most of the time (or so we hope).

Finally, the callback function that we supply to `RequestAnimationFrame` will be passed a timestamp value in the form of a `DOMHighResTimeStamp` type. This timestamp represents the time when the callbacks registered with `RequestAnimationFrame` get triggered in a given cycle. We can use this value to calculate the delta time since the previous frame, thus breaking our game loop out of the time-space continuum, which we'll discuss next.

Time-based game loop

Now that we have an effective way to update our game as fast as the underlying hardware is able to, we just need to control the rate at which the update happens. One option would be to ensure that the game loop doesn't execute again until at least some time has elapsed. This way we will not update more often than we know we have to. The other option is to calculate how long the previous update took and send that number into the update function so that it can move everything relative to that time difference:

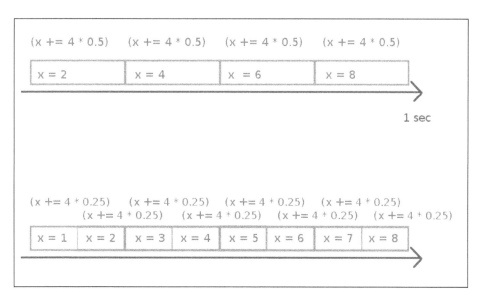

As illustrated in the preceding figure, if we update the game twice as fast in one browser or device, then the time taken to update a single frame (also known as the **delta time**) will be half as well. Using this delta as a factor in the physics update, we can make each update relative to how long it'll take to update a single frame. In other words, in the course of a whole second, we can either update the game a few times where each time the update is larger or we update the game many times during the same second, but each update would be much smaller. At the end of the second, we would have still moved the same distance.

Multiple game loops

Running a game smoothly and consistently across different CPUs is a victory on its own. Now that we're past that, let's think about how we can actually achieve it across the client and the server.

On the browser, we can run the game for the user using requestAnimationFrame, as demonstrated earlier. On the server, however, there is no requestAnimationFrame. Worse yet, we can't quite send updates across the network to all participants at a full 60 updates per second. In theory, we could very well do that—maybe for a few seconds before the server heats up and melts down. In other words, running 60 updates per second for every game in the same server would cause tremendous load on the server. Thus, we will need to slow down the update's pace on the server.

First things first, though. Since there is no requestAnimationFrame in Node.js, we know that we can't use it. However, since the concrete implementation of the game loop for the game server is separate from the game client's, we can just choose another timer mechanism that Node offers.

Secondly, we need to have a second timer running in the server so that it can send updates to the clients at a much slower pace. If we actually try to send updates to every single client at 60 frames per second, we will likely overload the server very quickly and performance will decrease.

The solution to the client update problem is to send updates at a slower but consistent rate, allowing the server to be the ultimate authority on game state in a way that we can scale. Between updates from the server, if the game requires quicker updates, we can make the game client update itself in the best way it can; then, once it receives information from the server, we can fix the client state if needed.

There are two timer functions that are commonly used in Node.js as higher resolution replacements for setTimeout(). These are setImmediate() and process.nextTick(). The reason you will want to use one of these two functions instead of setTimeout() is because setTimeout() doesn't guarantee the delay you specify nor does it guarantee the order in which the events will be executed.

For a better alternative, we can use setImmediate to schedule a callback to run after every event that is currently sitting on the event queue. We could also use process. nextTick, which will schedule the callback to run right after the current block of code finishes its execution.

While `process.nextTick` might seem like the better option between the two, keep in mind that it will not give the CPU a chance to execute other code in the event queue (or allow the CPU to rest), causing execution to consume 100 percent of the CPU. Thus, for the particular use case of a game loop in your Node.js game simulation, you might be better off using `setImmediate`.

As mentioned before, there will be two timers or loops running in the game server. The first is the physics update loop, which will use `setImmediate` in an attempt to efficiently run at a full 60 fps. The second will be the client sync loop, which doesn't need to run as fast.

The purpose of the client sync loop is to authoritatively tell the clients what the real state of the game is so that each client can update itself. If we try to let the server adjust each client at every frame, we would have a very slow game and a very slow server. A simple, widely used solution is to only synchronize the clients a couple of times per second. In the mean time, each client can play the game locally and then make any necessary corrections when the server updates its state.

Implementing an authoritative server

The strategy that we'll use for this server will be to run two game loops for two different purposes. The first loop is the physics update, which we'll run close to the same frequency as the clients' loop. The second loop, which we'll refer to as the client sync loop, is run at a slower pace, and at each tick, it will send the entire game state to every connected client.

At this point, we'll only focus on getting the server working as we've described. The current implementation of the clients will continue to work as it did, managing the entire game logic locally. Any data a client receives from the server (using the game sync loop) will only be rendered. Later in the book, we'll discuss the concept of client prediction, where we'll use the input from the game sync loop as the actual input for the game's logic rather than just rendering it mindlessly.

Game server interface

The first thing to change from the current implementation of the game client will be to break the input and output points so that they can communicate with the socket layer in the middle. We can think of this as a programming interface that specifies how the server and clients will communicate.

For this, let's create a simple module in our project to serve as a poor man's enum since enums aren't available in JavaScript. Though the data in this module will not be immutable, it will give us the advantage since the IDE will automatically suggest values, correct us when we make a typing mistake, and put all of our intents in one place. By convention, any event that starts with the word *server_* represent actions for the server. From example, the event named `server_newRoom` asks the server to create a new room:

```
// ch3/snake-ch3/share/events.js

module.exports = {
    server_spawnFruit: 'server:spawnFruit',
    server_newRoom: 'server:newRoom',
    server_startRoom: 'server:startRoom',
    server_joinRoom: 'server:joinRoom',
    server_listRooms: 'server:listRooms',
    server_setPlayerKey: 'server:setPlayerKey',

    client_newFruit: 'client:newFruit',
    client_roomJoined: 'client:roomJoined',
    client_roomsList: 'client:roomsList',
    client_playerState: 'client:playerState'
};
```

We now use the string values defined in this module to register callbacks for and emit events to sockets in a consistent and predictable way between the client and the server. For example, when we emit an event named `modules.exports.server_spawnFruit`, we know that what is intended is that a message to be received by the server has the action name of `spawnFruit`. In addition, you'll notice that we'll use `socket.io` to abstract away the socket communication between the client and the server. If you're curious to get started with `socket.io` right now, feel free to skip ahead to the end of this chapter and read the *Socket.io* section.

```
var gameEvents = require('./share/events.js');

socket.on(gameEvents.server_spawnFruit, function(data){
    var pos = game.spawnFruit(data.roomId, data.maxWidth, data.
maxHeight);

    socket.emit(gameEvents.client_newFruit, pos);
});
```

In the given example, we first include our module into a `gameEvents` variable. We then register a callback function whenever a socket receives an `server_spawnFruit` event. Presumably, this code is in some server code, as indicated by the server keyword at the beginning of the key name. This callback function takes a data argument created by the client (whoever is sending the command on the other end of the socket). This data object has the data that is needed by the specific call to spawn a new fruit object for the game.

Next, we use the input data into the socket event to perform some task (in this case, we generate a random position where a fruit can be added in the game world). With this data on hand, we emit a socket command back to the client to send the position that we just generated.

Updating the game client

The first thing to change in the client code is to add different screens. At a minimum, we need two different screens. One of the screens will be the game board as we've implemented so far. The other is the lobby, which we'll discuss in more detail later. In brief, the lobby is an area where players go before they join a specific room, which we'll also discuss shortly.

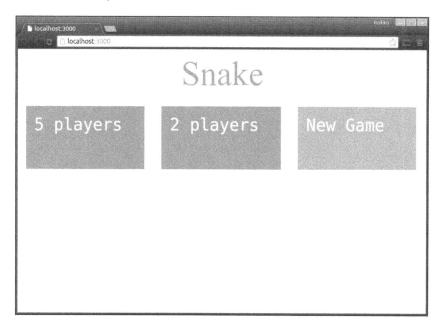

Once in the lobby, the player can choose to join an existing room or create and join a new room with no players in it.

In a perfect world, your game engine would offer great support for multiple screens. Since the sample game we're writing is not written in such a game engine, we'll just use basic HTML and CSS and write every screen along with any supporting props and widgets in the same HTML file that will be served up originally:

```
// ch3/snake-ch3/views/index.jade

extends layout

block content
  div#lobby
    h1 Snake
    div#roomList

div#main.hidden
  div#gameArea
    p#scoreA SCORE: <span>000000</span>
    p#gameOver.animated.pulse.hidden Game Over
    canvas#gameCanvas
    div#statsPanel

  script(src='/js/socket.io.js')
  script(src='/js/app.build.js')
```

There are only three blocks of code in the previous template. First, we have a `div` element with an ID of `lobby` inside which we dynamically add a list of available game rooms. Next, there is a `div` element with an ID of `main`, initially with a class of `hidden`, so that this screen is not visible initially. Finally, we include the `socket.io` library as well as our app.

The simplest way to bind to that HTML structure is to create module-wide global variables that reference each desired node. Once these references are in place, we can attach the necessary event listeners so that the player can interact with the interface:

```
// ch3/snake-ch3/share/app.client.js

var roomList = document.getElementById('roomList');
var screens = {
    main: document.getElementById('main'),
    lobby: document.getElementById('lobby')
};

// ...

socket.on(gameEvents.client_roomsList, function (rooms) {
```

```
    rooms.map(function (room) {
        var roomWidget = document.createElement('div');
        roomWidget.textContent = room.players.length + ' player';
        roomWidget.textContent += (room.players.length > 1 ? 's' :
'');

        roomWidget.addEventListener('click', function () {
            socket.emit(gameEvents.server_joinRoom, {
                    roomId: room.roomId,
                    playerId: player.id,
                    playerX: player.head.x,
                    playerY: player.head.y,
                    playerColor: player.color
                }
            );
        });

        roomList.appendChild(roomWidget);
    });

    var roomWidget = document.createElement('div');
    roomWidget.classList.add('newRoomWidget');
    roomWidget.textContent = 'New Game';

    roomWidget.addEventListener('click', function () {
        socket.emit(gameEvents.server_newRoom, {
            id: player.id,
            x: player.head.x,
            y: player.head.y,
            color: player.color,
            maxWidth: window.innerWidth,
            maxHeight: window.innerHeight
        });
    });

    roomList.appendChild(roomWidget);
});

socket.on(gameEvents.client_roomJoined, function (data) {
    // ...
    screens.lobby.classList.add('hidden');
    screens.main.classList.remove('hidden');
});
```

Since the initial game screen is the lobby, and the markup for the lobby is already visible, we don't do anything else to set it up. We simply register a socket callback to be invoked when we receive a list of available rooms and create individual HTML nodes with event listeners for each, attaching them to the DOM when we're ready.

Inside a different socket callback function, this time the one associated with the roomJoined custom event, we first make the lobby screen invisible, and then we make the main screen visible. We do this by adding and removing a CSS class named hidden, whose definition is shown in the following code snippet:

```
// ch3/snake-ch3/public/css/style.css

.hidden {
    display: none;
}
```

Understanding the game loop

The next set of changes that we'll need to make on the original game code is in the game class. As you'll remember, this class defines a basic game life cycle, exposing the functions update and render, which get implemented by whoever uses it.

Since the core of the game loop defined in this class (found in Game.prototype. loop) uses window.requestAnimationFrame, we'll need to get rid of that call since it will not be available in Node.js (or in any other environment outside the browser).

One technique that is commonly used to allow us the flexibility to write a single module that is used in both the browser and the server is to wrap the browser- and server-specific functions in a custom module.

Using Browserify, we can write two separate modules that wrap the environment-specific functionality but only reference a single one in the code. By configuring Browserify property, we can tell it to compile a different module whenever it sees a require statement for the custom wrapper module. For simplicity, we have only mentioned this capability here, but we will not get into it in this book. Instead, we will write a single component that automatically detects the environment it's under at runtime and responds accordingly.

```
// ch3/snake-ch3/share/tick.js
var tick = function () {
    var ticks = 0;
    var timer;

    if (typeof requestAnimationFrame === 'undefined') {
        timer = function (cb) {
```

```
                setTimeout(function () {
                    cb(++ticks);
                }, 0);
            }
        } else {
            timer = window.requestAnimationFrame;
        }

        return function (cb) {
            return timer(cb);
        }
    };

    module.exports = tick();
```

The tick component is made up of a function that returns one of the two functions, depending on the availability of window.requestAnimationFrame. This pattern might look somewhat confusing at first, but it offers the benefit that it only detects the environment once and then makes the environment-specific functionality every time after the initial setup.

Note that what we export from this module is a call to tick and not a mere reference. This way, when we require the module, what ends up being referenced in the client code is the function returned by tick. In a browser, this will be a reference to window.requestAnimationFrame, and in node, it'll be a function that calls setTimeout, by passing an incrementing number to it, similar to how the browser version of tick would.

Game client's game loop

Now that the abstract game loop class is ready for use in any environment, let's take a look at how we could refactor the existing client implementation so that it can be driven by sockets connected to the authoritative server.

Note how we no longer determine when a new fruit should be generated. All that we check for on the client is how we might move the player's character. We could let the server tell us where the snake is at each frame, but that would overload the application. We could also only render the main snake when the server syncs its state, but that would make the entire game seem really slow.

What we do instead is just copy the entire logic here and ignore what the server says about it when we sync. Later, we'll talk about client prediction; at that point, we'll add some logic here to correct any discrepancies that we find when the server syncs with us.

```
// ch3/snake-ch3/share/app.client.js

game.onUpdate = function (delta) {
    // The client no longer checks if the player has eaten a fruit.
    // This task has now become the server's jurisdiction.
    player.update(delta);
    player.checkCollision();

    if (player.head.x < 0) {
        player.head.x = parseInt(renderer.canvas.width / player.width,
10);
    }

    if (player.head.x > parseInt(renderer.canvas.width / player.width,
10)) {
        player.head.x = 0;
    }

    if (player.head.y < 0) {
        player.head.y = parseInt(renderer.canvas.height / player.
height, 10);
    }

    if (player.head.y > parseInt(renderer.canvas.height / player.
height, 10)) {
        player.head.y = 0;
    }

    if (fruits.length > 0) {
        if (player.head.x === fruits[0].x && player.head.y ===
fruits[0].y) {
            fruits = [];
            player.grow();
        }
    }
};
```

Game server's game loop

This is where things get exciting. Before we implement the game loop for the server-side code, we'll first need to implement an API that the client will use to query the server and issue other commands.

One of the benefits of using `express` in this project is that it works so well with `Socket.io`. Without stealing any thunder from the section later in this chapter that is dedicated to Socket.io, this is how our main server script will look like:

```
// ch3/snake-ch3/app.js

// ...

var io = require('socket.io')();
var gameEvents = require('./share/events.js');
var game = require('./server/app.js');

var app = express();
app.io = io;

// ...

io.on('connection', function(socket){
    // when a client requests a new room, create one, and assign
    // that client to this new room immediately.
    socket.on(gameEvents.server_newRoom, function(data){
        var roomId = game.newRoom(data.maxWidth, data.maxHeight);
        game.joinRoom(roomId, this, data.id, data.x, data.y, data.
color);
    });

    // when a client requests to join an existing room, assign that
    // client to the room whose roomId is provided.
    socket.on(gameEvents.server_joinRoom, function(data){
        game.joinRoom(data.roomId, this, data.playerId, data.playerX,
data.playerY, data.playerColor);
    });

    // when a client wishes to know what all the available rooms are,
    // send back a list of roomIds, along with how many active players
    // are in each room.
    socket.on(gameEvents.server_listRooms, function(){
        var rooms = game.listRooms();
        socket.emit(gameEvents.client_roomsList, rooms);
    });
});
```

Adding to the default Express `app.js` script, we import `Socket.io`, the game events module that we defined earlier, and the game application that we will discuss throughout the rest of the chapter.

Next, after we've finished setting up Express, we set up our socket communication with the clients. The first step is to wait until a connection has been established, which will give us access to an individual socket that is bound to an individual client.

Once we have a live socket, we configure all the events we care about by registering custom event listeners to each event. You will notice that some of the sample event listeners mentioned previously also emit events back to the requesting socket, while others simply call methods on the game object. The difference between the two scenarios is that when we only need to talk to a single client (the requesting client), we contact that socket directly from the event listener. There are situations, however, when we might wish to talk to all the sockets connected to the same room. When this is the case, we must let the game object alert all the players that it needs since it will know who all are the clients that belong to a given room.

Lobby and room system

The concepts of game rooms and a lobby are central to multiplayer gaming. In order to understand how it works, think about the game server as a building in which people go in order to play games together.

Before entering the building, a player may stand in front of the building and enjoy the beauty of the outside walls. In our metaphor, staring at the front of the building would be the equivalent of being greeted by a splash screen that introduces the game.

Upon entering the building, the player may or may not see some options from which to make a choice, such as a listing of the available floor to which he or she may want to go. In some games, you can choose the type of game to play as well as a difficulty level. Think of this as taking an elevator to a specific floor.

Finally, you arrive at a lobby. Similar to the way a lobby works in real life, in multiplayer games, the lobby is a special room that multiple players go to before entering a specific room where the playing takes place. In the lobby, you can see what the available rooms are and then choose one to join.

Once you have decided which room you'd like to join, you can now enter that room and participate in an existing game with other players. Alternatively, you can join an empty room and wait for others to join you there.

Typically, there is never an empty room in multiplayer games. Every room has at least one player in it, and every player can belong to one room at a time. Once all players have left the room, the game server would delete the room and release the associated resources.

Implementing the lobby

With the basic understanding of a lobby, we can implement it in a number of ways. Generally speaking, a lobby is actually a special room that all players join before they end up at a room where they'll play a particular game.

One way to implement this is to keep track of all socket connections in your server as an array. For all practical purposes, that array of sockets is your lobby. Once a player connects to the lobby (in other words, once a player has connected to your server), he or she can communicate with other players and possibly be an observing participant in a conversation between other players in the lobby.

In our case, the lobby is simple and to the point. A player is assigned to the lobby automatically upon starting the game. Once in the lobby, the player queries the server for a list of available rooms. From there, the player can issue a socket command to join an existing room or create a new one:

```
// ch3/snake-ch3/server/app.js

var Game = require('./../share/game.js');
var gameEvents = require('./../share/events.js');
var Room = require('./room.js');

// ...

/** @type {Array.<Room>} */
var rooms = [];

module.exports = {
    newRoom: function(maxWidth, maxHeight){
        var room = new Room(FPS, maxWidth, maxHeight);
        rooms.push(room);
        return rooms.length - 1;
    },

    listRooms: function(){
        return rooms.map(function(room, index) {
            return {
                roomId: index,
```

```
                         players: room.players.map(function(player){
                    return {
                        id: player.snake.id,
                        x: player.snake.head.x,
                        y: player.snake.head.y,
                        color: player.snake.color
                    };
                })
            };
        });
    },

    joinRoom: function(roomId, socket, playerId, playerX, playerY,
playerColor) {
        var room = rooms[roomId];
        var snake = new Snake(playerId, playerX, playerY, playerColor,
1, 1);
        room.join(snake, socket);

        socket.emit(gameEvents.client_roomJoined, {roomId: roomId});
    },
};
```

Remember that our main server script exposed an interface that sockets could use to communicate with the game server. The previously mentioned script is the backend service with which the interface communicated. The actual sockets connected to the server are stored in and managed by Socket.io.

The list of available rooms is implemented as an array of Room objects, which we'll look at in detail in the next section. Note that every room will need at least two things. First, a room will need a way to group players and run the game with those same players. Second, a room will need a way for both the client and server to uniquely identify each individual room.

The two simple approaches to identify the rooms individually are to ensure that each room object has an ID property, which would need to be unique across the entire game space, or we could use the array index where the room is stored.

For simplicity, we've chosen the second. Keep in mind that, should we delete a room and splice it off the rooms array, the room ID that some players have may now point to the wrong room.

For example, suppose there are three rooms in the array so that the room ID for the rooms are 0, 1, and 2 respectively. Suppose that each of these rooms have several players participating in a game there. Finally, imagine that all the players in room ID 0 leave the game. If we splice that first room off the array (stored at index 0), then the room that used to be the second element in the array (formerly stored at index 1) would be shifted down to the front of the array (index 0). The third element in the array would also change and would be stored at index 1 instead of index 2. Thus, players who used to be in rooms 1 and 2 respectively will now report back to the game server with those same room IDs, but the server will report the first room as the second one, and the second room will not exist. Therefore, we must avoid deleting empty rooms by splicing them off the rooms array. Remember that the largest integer that JavaScript can represent is 2^{53} (which equals 9,007,199,254,740,992), so we will not run out of slots in the array if we simply add new rooms to the end of the rooms array.

Implementing the rooms

The game room is a module that implements the game class and runs the game loop. This module looks fairly similar to the client game as it has references to the player and fruit objects and updates the game state at each game tick.

One difference you will notice is that there is no render phase in the server. In addition, the room will need to expose a few methods so that the server application can managed it as needed. Since each room has references to all the players in it and every player in the server is represented by a socket, the room can contact every player who is connected to it:

```
// ch3/snake-ch3/server/room.js

var Game = require('./../share/game.js');
var Snake = require('./../share/snake.js');
var Fruit = require('./../share/fruit.js');
var keys = require('./../share/keyboard.js');
var gameEvents = require('./../share/events.js');

/** @type {Game} game */
var game = null, gameUpdateRate = 1, gameUpdates = 0;
var players = [], fruits = [], fruitColor = '#c00';
var fruitDelay = 1500, lastFruit = 0, fruitDelta = 0;

var Room = function (fps, worldWidth, worldHeight) {
    var self = this;
    game = new Game(fps);
```

```
        game.onUpdate = function (delta) {
            var now = process.hrtime()[1];
            if (fruits.length < 1) {
                fruitDelta = now - lastFruit;

                if (fruitDelta >= fruitDelay) {
                    var pos = {
                        x: parseInt(Math.random() * worldWidth, 10),
                        y: parseInt(Math.random() * worldHeight, 10)
                    };

                    self.addFruit(pos);
                    players.map(function(player){
                        player.socket.emit(gameEvents.client_newFruit,
pos);
                    });
                }
            }

            players.map(function (player) {
                player.snake.update(delta);
                player.snake.checkCollision();

                if (player.snake.head.x < 0) {
                    player.snake.head.x = worldWidth;
                }

                if (player.snake.head.x > worldWidth) {
                    player.snake.head.x = 0;
                }

                if (player.snake.head.y < 0) {
                    player.snake.head.y = worldHeight;
                }

                if (player.snake.head.y > worldHeight) {
                    player.snake.head.y = 0;
                }

                if (fruits.length > 0) {
                    if (player.snake.head.x === fruits[0].x
                        && player.snake.head.y === fruits[0].y) {
                        fruits = [];
                        player.snake.grow();
```

```
                          }
                      }
                });

            if (++gameUpdates % gameUpdateRate === 0) {
                gameUpdates = 0;
                var data = players.map(function(player){
                    return player.snake;
                });
                players.map(function(player){
                    player.socket.emit(gameEvents.client_playerState,
data);
                });

                lastFruit = now;
            }
        };
    };

Room.prototype.start = function () {
    game.start();
};

Room.prototype.addFruit = function (pos) {
    fruits[0] = new Fruit(pos.x, pos.y, fruitColor, 1, 1);
};

Room.prototype.join = function (snake, socket) {
    if (players.indexOf(snake.id) < 0) {
        players.push({
            snake: snake,
            socket: socket
        });
    }
};

Room.prototype.getPlayers = function(){
    return players;
};

module.exports = Room;
```

Note that the players array holds a list of object literals that contain a reference to a snake object as well as the actual socket. This way both resources are together in the same logical place. Whenever we need to ping every player in the room, we can simply map over the player's array and then access the socket through `player.socket.emit`.

In addition, note that the sync loop is placed inside the main game loop, but we only trigger the logic inside the sync loop whenever a certain amount of frames have elapsed. The goal is to only synchronize all the clients every so often.

Matching players within game rooms

After we have broken down the various concepts into simple fundamentals, you will see that implementing each module is not as complicated as they may have sounded at first. Player matching is one such example.

There are different ways in which you might want to match players in a game room. While our sample game doesn't do any complex matching (we allow players to blindly match themselves), you should know that there are more options here.

The following are some ideas about how you might go about matching players into the same game world. Keep in mind that there are third-party services, such as Google's Play Services API, that you can use to help you with these.

Inviting friends into your world

One of the most engaging ways to match players leverages the social aspect of today's world. By integrating with a social network service (or using your own social network populated by your players), you can give a player the option to invite a friend to play with them.

While this can be a fun experience, it goes without saying that both players must be online at the same time for the game to be played. Often, this means that when a player sends an invite to his or her friend, an email is sent to the friend with information about the invitation. Whenever the friend joins the game room and both players are ready, the fun can begin.

A variation of this technique is to only show available friends (that is, friends who are already online and either in the lobby or in a game room). This way play can begin immediately or as soon as the friend exits the current game.

Auto-matching

Perhaps, you don't have a social network to leverage, or perhaps, the player doesn't care who the opponents are. When you want the player to be able to just get in and play a quick game, auto-matching is a great option.

There are more specific ways to automatically match players (for example, automatically match players based on their skills or some other criteria), but in its most basic form, you would need to create a private room for the first player (by private room, I mean a room that isn't listed for any player to join—only the game server knows about it), then wait for a matching player to join that room.

Skill-based matching

Another common way that players are matched into the same game room is by grouping players together based on their skill level. The way you keep track of a player's skill level can be determined in at least three ways— namely, by asking the user what his or her skill level is, by monitoring them during a single session, or by persisting the player's information across multiple sessions.

The first option is the easiest to implement. A common way in which this is done is by displaying a menu with three or more options asking the player to choose from the options, such as amateur, advanced, and rock star. Based on this selection, you will then try to match other players from the same group.

One possible benefit of this approach is that a new player with no past history with the game (from the point of view of the server) can start playing more advanced players right away. On the other hand, the same feature can be considered to be a downside to the approach as truly advanced players who may only wish to play with equally skilled players might get frustrated by being matched up against poor players who claim to possess a higher skill level than they really qualify for.

The second option is to start everyone at the same level (or randomly assign the first skill level for incoming players). Then, as more games are played, the application can keep track of each player's wins and losses along with other metadata about each player to allow you to bucket each player into a current skill level.

For example, a player may start the game in a beginner's room. After winning two games and losing none, you can then put this player in a advanced room. After the player has played additional two or three games and has two or three more victories under their belt, you can now consider that player to be in the super-advanced level.

The obvious downside to this approach is that it makes the assumption that an individual player will stay logged in long enough to play multiple games. Depending on the type of game you're designing, most players won't even be logged in to finish a single playing session.

However, if your game is a good candidate for this type of approach (where a single game doesn't last longer than a few minutes), then this matching technique works out quite well because you won't need to write any long term persistence logic or need to authenticate users.

Finally, you can keep track of a player's skill level by persisting their information in some form of backend database. In most cases, this will require players to have individual accounts, which will need to be authenticated before the play begins.

Again, in some cases, you might want to use an existing third-party service to authenticate players, and possibly persist information you generate about them in the service itself.

While this can get pretty elaborate and engaging, the basic concept is simple — calculate some sort of score that can be used to deduce a player's skill level and store that information away somewhere in a way that it can be retrieved later. From this point of view, you can possibly implement this persistence by storing the player's current skill level locally using HTML5's local storage API. The main drawback of doing this would be that this data would be stuck in the player's machine, so if the player uses a different machine (or wipes out their local storage data), you won't have access to the data.

Socket.io

In *Chapter 1, Getting Started with Multiplayer Game Programming*, we implemented the first demo game using native HTML5 sockets. Although WebSockets are still totally awesome, they are unfortunately still heavily dependent on the specific browser the player uses.

Today, every modern browser ships with a complete implementation of WebSockets, especially on mobile devices where the world seems to be converging. However, for the possible exception where the user's browser doesn't quite support WebSockets but does support canvas (or whatever other HTML5 API you game uses), Socket.io comes to the rescue.

In short, Socket.io is an open source library that offers a fantastic level of abstraction over sockets. Not only this, Socket.io also makes it super easy to implement the backend service that the frontend socket clients will consume.

To implement the server-side code is as easy as specifying the port on which the connection will be and then implementing callbacks for events in which you're interested.

Now, this book is not a comprehensive guide for those wanting to master every aspect of Socket.io and will not be too descriptive for a lot of features that are offered by the library. However, you might find it useful to know that Socket.io offers amazing client-side support. In other words, if the browser using the socket doesn't implement the WebSockets specification, then Socket.io will fallback to some other technique that can be used to communicate with the server asynchronously. While some of these techniques may be too slow for real-time gaming (for example, Socket. io will eventually fallback to using HTML iFrames to communicate with the server if nothing else is supported by the browser), it is good to know just how powerful the library is.

Installing Socket.io

We will bring Socket.io into our project through NPM. Be sure to stay close to the version used in this book (which is 1.3.5), as some of the methods or configurations might vary.

```
npm install socket.io --save
npm install socket.io-client –save
```

Again, since we're using the Express framework to ease the effort of creating the Node.js server, we'll integrate Socket.io with Express.

```
// ch3/snake-ch3/app.js

var express = require('express');
var io = require('socket.io')();

// ...

var app = express();
app.io = io;

// ...

io.on('connection', function(socket){
        console.log('New client connected. Socket ready!');
    });
});
```

The first thing we need to do is `require` Socket.io together with Express and all your other dependencies for the server script. We then add Socket.io to the Express instance by taking advantage of JavaScript's dynamic nature. We do this because Socket.io is not fully set up yet since we'll need access to the HTTP server that Express uses. In our case, as is the current standard today, we use Express Version 4.9.0 along with express-generator, which generates a file under <project-name>/ bin/www where the low-level server setup takes place. This is where we integrate Socket.io into Express, by attaching the same server used by Express into our Socket. io instance.

```
// ch3/snake-ch3/bin/www

#!/usr/bin/env node
var debug = require('debug')('snake-ch3');
var app = require('../app');

app.set('port', process.env.PORT || 3000);

var server = app.listen(app.get('port'), function() {
  debug('Express server listening on port ' + server.address().port);
});

app.io.attach(server);
```

Client-side Socket.io

The last step is to use the Socket.io library in our client JavaScript. Here, there are only two simple steps that you must be certainly used to by now if you've ever done any JavaScript programming at all.

First, we copy the client-side library into our public directory so that we can include it into our client code. To do this, copy the `ch3/snake-ch3/node_modules/socket.io-client/socket.io.js` file into `ch3/snake-ch3/public/js/socket.io.js`. Next, include the library in your HTML file using a script tag.

To start using the socket in your client code, all you need to do is instantiate it by requiring it with the domain where the server is running.

```
// ch3/snake-ch3/share/app.client.js

var socket = require('socket.io-client')(window.location.origin);

// ...

socket.on('connect', function () {
    socket.emit(gameEvents.server_listRooms);
});
```

Now, the socket will attempt to connect to your server right away and asynchronously. Once it does this, the connect event will fire and the corresponding callback will be fired as well, and you would know that the socket is ready to be used. From then on you can start emitting events to the other end of the socket.

Summary

Hopefully, this chapter got you excited about the unique aspects of multiplayer game development. We took an existing single-player snake game and broke it apart into an authoritative server component and a socket-driven frontend component. We used Socket.io to link the game client and server together in a very seamless integration with Express. We also discussed the concept of a game lobby and game rooms as well as the way to match players into the same game world.

In the next chapter, we will improve our Snake game by adding reduced network latency with client prediction and correction as well as input interpolation. We will also fix the game server's game loop for smoother and more efficient game play.

4
Reducing Network Latency

Now that we have a working game that allows the presence of multiple players in the same or multiple game rooms, we will iterate and take care of a very important issue in online games, namely, network latency. Given the fact that you will need to think about this problem for many years to come, we will be very focused on the topics covered in this chapter.

In this chapter, we will discuss the following principles and concepts:

- Dealing with network latency in multiplayer games
- Implementing a local game server in the client
- Client-side prediction
- Interpolating real positions to correct bad predictions

Dealing with network latency

Although you may well be one of the happy citizens out there with a gigabit internet connection, you should know that most of the world is certainly not as fortunate. Thus, some of the most important things to keep in mind when developing online multiplayer games are that not all players will have the same network speed and not all players will have high-speed connections.

The main takeaway point that you need to remember from this section is that, as long as there is a network between your players and the game server (or between two players connected directly to each other), there will be latency.

It is true that not all games need near instantaneous response times over the network, for example, turn-based games such as Chess, or our implementation of Snake, since the game tick is much slower than most action games. However, for a real-time, fast-paced game, even a small latency of, say, 50 ms, can make the game very jerky and annoying to play.

Imagine this for a moment. You press the right arrow key on the keyboard. Your game client tells the server that your intent is to move to the right. The server finally gets your message 50 ms later, runs its update cycle, and tells you to place your character at the position (23, 42). Finally, another 50 ms later, your client receives the message from the server, and a whole tenth of a second after you pressed the key on the keyboard, your player begins to move to your desired location.

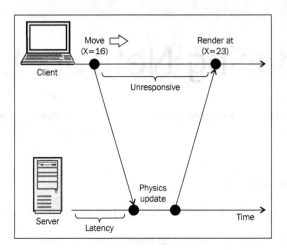

As mentioned in the previous chapters, the most commonly used solution to the network latency problem is to change the client logic so that it can respond to user input immediately, while updating the server about its input at the same time. The authoritative server then updates its own game state based on the input from each client and finally sends out its version of the current state of the game world to all of the clients. These clients can then update themselves so that they are in sync with the server and the process continues.

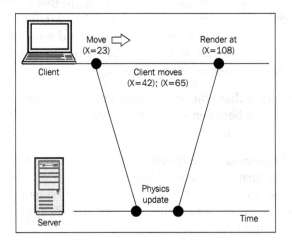

Thus, as you may have realized, the goal is not at all to get rid of latency since this is physically impossible, but merely to hide it behind a constantly updating game so that the player has the illusion that the game is being updated by the server in real time.

As long as the player feels that the game is responsive and behaves as the player expects it to, for all practical purposes, you have solved the network latency issue. With every communication with the server (or from the server to the client), ask yourself where the latency is and how you can hide it by keeping the game going while the packets travel across the wire.

Synchronizing clients in lockstep

So far, we've discussed the client-server structure where the server is the ultimate authority on the game, and clients have little or no authority over the game's logic. In other words, clients simply take in any input from the player and pass it along to the server. Once the server sends out updated positions to the clients, the game state is rendered by the clients.

One other model that is commonly used in online multiplayer games is the lockstep method. In this method, a client tells the server about any input received from the player as often as it can. The server then broadcasts this input to all other clients. The clients in turn use the input state for each participant in the next update cycle, and in theory, everyone ends up with the same game state. Each time the server takes a lockstep (runs physics update from the input data from each client), we call it a turn.

In order for the server to remain as the ultimate authority over the game, an update cycle is also run in the server's simulation, and the output of the simulation is also broadcasted to the clients. If a client's updated state differs from the one sent by the server, the client takes the server's data to be correct and updates itself accordingly.

Fixed-time step

The first thing that we'll update in our server's code is the game loop, and the first thing that it'll do differently is that it will no longer have the concept of delta times. In addition, we will need to queue up all input from each client between update cycles so that we have the data to update the game state with, when we run the physics update.

Since we're now using a consistent time step, we have no need to keep track of delta times on the server. As a result, the server also has no concept of delta times from the clients' perspective.

For example, imagine a racing game where a player is driving at, say, 300 pixels per second. Suppose this particular client is running the game at a frequency of 60 frames per second. Provided that the car maintained a steady speed during the entire second, then after 60 frames, the car will have travelled 300 pixels. Additionally, during each frame the car will have travelled an average of 5 pixels.

Now, suppose that the server's game loop is configured to run at a frequency of 10 frames per second, or once every 100 milliseconds. The car will now travel further per frame (30 pixels instead of 5 pixels), but in the end, it will also be 300 pixels further than where it started one second ago.

60 fps → speed=0.31px (every 16.66ms)	0	5px	10px	15px	...	300px
	0	1	2	3		60

10 fps (every 100ms)	0	30px	...	300px
	0	1		10

In summary, while the clients will still need to track how long it takes to process a single frame in order for all the clients to run at the same speed, regardless of how fast or slow different computers run the game loop, the server's game loop doesn't care about any of this because it doesn't need to.

```
// ch4/snake-ch4/share/tick.js

var tick = function (delay) {
    var _delay = delay;
    var timer;

    if (typeof requestAnimationFrame === 'undefined') {
        timer = function (cb) {
            setImmediate(function () {
                cb(_delay);
            }, _delay);
        }
    } else {
        timer = window.requestAnimationFrame;
    }

    return function (cb) {
        return timer(cb);
    }
};

module.exports = tick;
```

Here, we first update our tick module that we built for the purpose of reusing code in the server code as well as in the code that is shipped to the browser. Note the use of setImmediate instead of setTimeout, which will perform theoretically faster since the callback is scheduled earlier in the execution queue.

In addition, observe how we export the wrapper tick function instead of the closure that it returns. This way we can configure the server's timer before exporting the function.

Finally, since the delta time is now predictable and consistent, we no longer need the tick's variable to simulate the passage of time. Now, we can just pass the interval value directly into the callback function after each tick.

```javascript
// ch4/snake-ch4/share/game.js

var tick = require('./tick.js');
tick = tick(100);

var Game = function (fps) {
    this.fps = fps;
    this.delay = 1000 / this.fps;
    this.lastTime = 0;
    this.raf = 0;

    this.onUpdate = function (delta) {
    };

    this.onRender = function () {
    };
};

Game.prototype.update = function (delta) {
    this.onUpdate(delta);
};

Game.prototype.render = function () {
    this.onRender();
};

Game.prototype.loop = function (now) {
    this.raf = tick(this.loop.bind(this));

    var delta = now - this.lastTime;
    if (delta >= this.delay) {
```

```
        this.update(delta);
        this.render();
        this.lastTime = now;
    }
};
```

The only difference that you will notice here is that the `tick` module is called with the frequency it is being passed in, so we can configure how fast we wish it to run.

You may wonder why we selected the possibly arbitrary number of 10 updates per second for the server's game loop. Remember that our goal is to make our players believe that they're actually playing an awesome game together with other players.

The way in which we can achieve this illusion of real-time game play is by carefully hand-tuning the server to update fast enough so that the accuracy is not too far off and slow enough so that the clients can move in such a way that the lag is not too noticeable.

You need to find the balance between the authoritative server that provides accurate game state versus the client's ability to provide a responsive experience to the player. The more often you update the clients with data from the server's update cycle, the less accurate your simulation will be; this depend on how much data the simulation had to process and possibly drop data along the way in order to keep up with the high update frequency. Similarly, the less often you update the clients with data from the server's update cycle, the less responsive the client will feel, since it'll need to wait longer on the server before it knows for sure what the correct game state should be.

Synchronizing the clients

As the server consistently pushes out updates about the current state of the game world, we need a way for the clients to consume and make use of this data. A simple way to achieve this is to hold the latest server state outside the game class and update itself whenever the data is available since it won't be present every update `tick`.

```
// ch4/snake-ch4/share/app.client.js

// All of the requires up top
// ...

var serverState = {};
```

```
// ...

socket.on(gameEvents.client_playerState, function(data){
    otherPlayers = data.filter(function(_player){

        if (_player.id == player.id) {
            serverState = _player;
            return false;
        }

        _player.width = BLOCK_WIDTH;
        _player.height = BLOCK_HEIGHT;
        _player.head.x = parseInt(_player.head.x / BLOCK_WIDTH,
10);
        _player.head.y = parseInt(_player.head.y / BLOCK_HEIGHT,
10);
        _player.pieces = _player.pieces.map(function(piece){
            piece.x = parseInt(piece.x / BLOCK_WIDTH, 10);
            piece.y = parseInt(piece.y / BLOCK_HEIGHT, 10);

            return piece;
        });

        return true;
    });
});
```

Here, we declare the `serverState` variable as a module-wide global. Then, we modify the socket listener that grabs the state of all other players when the server updates that, but now, we look for the reference to the player that represents the hero here, and store that in the global `serverState` variable.

With this global state on hand, we can now check for its existence during the update method of the client and act accordingly. If the state is not there at the beginning of a given update cycle, we update the client as before. If the world state from the server is in fact available to us at the beginning of the next client update `tick`, we can synchronize the client's positions with the server instead.

```
// ch4/snake-ch4/share/app.client.js

game.onUpdate = function (delta) {

    if (serverState.id) {
        player.sync(serverState);
```

```
            // On subsequent ticks, we may not in sync any more,
            // so let's get rid of the serverState after we use it
            if (player.isSyncd()) {
                serverState = {};
            }
        } else {
            player.update(delta);
            player.checkCollision();

            if (player.head.x < 0) {
                player.head.x = parseInt(renderer.canvas.width /
    player.width, 10);
            }

            if (player.head.x > parseInt(renderer.canvas.width /
    player.width, 10)) {
                player.head.x = 0;
            }

            if (player.head.y < 0) {
                player.head.y = parseInt(renderer.canvas.height /
    player.height, 10);
            }

            if (player.head.y > parseInt(renderer.canvas.height /
    player.height, 10)) {
                player.head.y = 0;
            }
        }
    };
```

The actual implementation of `Player.prototype.sync` will depend on our strategy for error correction, which is described in the next couple of sections. Eventually, we'll want to incorporate both teleportation and interpolation, but for now, we'll just check whether any error correction is even necessary.

```
// ch4/snake-ch4/share/snake.js

var Snake = function (id, x, y, color_hex, width, height) {
    this.id = id;
    this.color = color_hex;
    this.head = {
        x: x,
        y: y
    };
```

```
        this.pieces = [this.head];
        this.width = width || 16;
        this.height = height || 16;
        this.readyToGrow = false;
        this.input = {};

        this.inSync = true;
    };

    Snake.prototype.isSyncd = function(){
        return this.inSync;
    };

    Snake.prototype.sync = function(serverState) {
        var diffX = serverState.head.x - this.head.x;
        var diffY = serverState.head.y - this.head.y;

        if (diffX === 0 && diffY === 0) {
            this.inSync = true;
            return true;
        }

        this.inSync = false;

        // TODO: Implement error correction strategies here

        return false;
    };
```

The changes to the snake class are pretty straightforward. We add a flag to let us know whether we still need to synchronize with the server state after a single update cycle. This is necessary because when we decide to interpolate between two points, we'll need multiple update cycles to get there. Next, we add a method that we can call to verify whether the player is (or isn't) in sync with the server, which determines how the snake updated the given frame. Finally, we add a method that performs the actual synchronization. Right now, we simply check whether there is a need to update our position. As we discuss different error correction strategies, we'll update the Snake.prototype.sync method to make use of them.

Predicting the future with a local game server

The strategy that we will use in order to make our clients responsive, yet bound to the authoritative server, is that we will act on the input that we receive from the player while we tell the server about the input. In other words, we will need to take the player's input and predict what will happen to our game state as a result, while we wait to hear back from the server with the actual output of the player's action.

Client-side prediction can be summarized as your best guess about what should happen between authoritative updates. In other words, we can reuse some of the server code that updates the game world on the client-side so that our guess about what the output should be from the player's input is pretty much the same as what the server will simulate.

Reporting user input

The first thing that we'll change is the control mechanism on the client side. Instead of simply keeping track of our position locally, we'll also inform the server that the player has pressed a key.

```
// ch4/snake-ch4/share/app.client.js

document.body.addEventListener('keydown', function (e) {
    var key = e.keyCode;

    switch (key) {
        case keys.ESC:
            game.stop();
            break;

        case keys.SPACEBAR:
            game.start();
            break;

        case keys.LEFT:
        case keys.RIGHT:
        case keys.UP:
        case keys.DOWN:
            player.setKey(key);
            socket.emit(gameEvents.server_setPlayerKey, {
                    roomId: roomId,
```

```
                    playerId: player.id,
                    keyCode: key
                }
            );

            break;
        }
    });
```

Of course, doing this directly in the event handler's callback might quickly overwhelm the server, so be sure to time this upward reporting. One way to do this is to use the `tick` update to contact the server.

```
// ch4/snake-ch4/share/app.client.js

game.onUpdate = function (delta) {
    player.update(delta);
    player.checkCollision();

    // …

    socket.emit(gameEvents.server_setPlayerKey, {
            roomId: roomId,
            playerId: player.id,
            keyState: player.input
        }
    );
};
```

Now, we update the server at the same frequency that we update our local simulation, which is not a bad idea. However, you might also consider leaving all networking logic outside of the `game` class (`update` and `render` methods) so that the networking aspects of the game is abstracted out of the game altogether.

For this, we can put the socket emitter right back in the controller's event handler; however, instead of calling the server right away, we can use a timer to keep the updates consistent. The idea is that, when a key is pressed, we call the server right away with the update. If the user pushes a key again before some time has gone by, we wait a certain amount of time before calling the server again.

```
// ch4/snake-ch4/share/app.client.js

// All of the requires up top
// …
```

```
var inputTimer = 0;
var inputTimeoutPeriod = 100;

// …

document.body.addEventListener('keydown', function (e) {
    var key = e.keyCode;

    switch (key) {
        case keys.ESC:
            game.stop();
            break;

        case keys.SPACEBAR:
            game.start();
            break;

        case keys.LEFT:
        case keys.RIGHT:
        case keys.UP:
        case keys.DOWN:
            player.setKey(key);

            if (inputTimer === 0) {
                inputTimer = setTimeout(function(){
                    socket.emit(gameEvents.server_setPlayerKey, {
                        roomId: roomId,
                        playerId: player.id,
                        keyCode: key
                    }
                    );
                }, inputTimeoutPeriod);
            } else {
                clearTimeout(inputTimer);
                inputTimer = 0;
            }

            break;
    }
});
```

Here, the `inputTimer` variable is a reference to the timer that we created with `setTimeout`, which we can be canceled at any moment until the timer is actually fired. This way, if the player presses many keys really fast (or holds a key down for a while), we can ignore the additional events.

One side effect of this implementation is that, if the player holds down the same key for a long time, the timer that wraps the call to `socket.emit` will continue to be canceled, and the server will never be notified of subsequent key presses. While this may seem like a potential problem at first, it is actually a very welcome feature. Firstly, in the case of this particular game where pressing the same key two or more times has no effect, we really don't need to report the additional presses to the server. Secondly (and this holds true for any other type of game as well), we can let the server assume that, after the player presses the right arrow key, the right key is still being pressed until we tell the server otherwise. Since our `Snake` game doesn't have a concept of a key being released (meaning that the snake will constantly move in the direction of the last key press until we change its direction), the server will continue to move the snake in a given direction until we press a different key and tell the server to move it in the new direction.

Error correction

Once the server has every player's input state, positions, and intents, it can take a lockstep turn and update the entire game world. Since at the time when an individual player makes a move, he or she only knows about what is happening in that particular client, one thing that could happen is that another player could play in their local client in such a way that there is a conflict between the two players. Maybe, there was only one fruit and both players attempted to get to it at the same time, or it is possible that another player ran into you, and you're now going to be taking some damage.

This is where the authoritative server comes into play and puts all the clients on the same page. Whatever each client predicted in isolation should now match what the server has determined so that everyone can see the game world in the same state.

Here is a classic example of a situation where network latency can get in the way of a fun multiplayer experience. Let's imagine that, two players (player A and player B) start heading for the same fruit. According to each player's simulation, they're both coming from opposite directions and headed for the fruit, which is now only a few frames away. If neither player changes direction, they would both arrive at the fruit at the exact same frame. Suppose that, in the frame before player A eats the fruit, he decided to change direction for whatever reason. Since player B doesn't get player A's updated state and position from the server for a few frames, he might think that player A was indeed going to eat the fruit, so player B's simulation would show player A eating the fruit and getting points for it.

Given the previous scenario, what should player B's simulation do when the server sends the next turn's output that shows that player A swerved away from the fruit and didn't earn any points? Indeed, the two states are now out of sync (between player B's simulation and the server), so player B should get better synchronized with the server.

Play through the intent, but not the outcome

A common way to handle the scenario that was mentioned previously is to include some sort of animation that a client can start right away based on its current knowledge of the player's intent and the current state of the game world. In our specific case, when player B thinks that player A is about to grab the fruit and earn some points, his or her simulation could start an animation sequence that would indicate that player A is about to level up by eating a fruit. Then, when the server responds back and confirms that player A didn't actually eat the fruit, player B's client can fall back to some secondary animation that would represent that the fruit was untouched.

Those of you who are fans of **Halo** might have noticed this in action when you attempted to throw a grenade in the game during an online session with your mates. When a client decides to toss a hand grenade in Halo, the client will inform the server about this intent right away. The server will then run a bunch of tests and checks to make sure that this is a legal move. Finally, the server will respond back to the client and inform it whether it is allowed to continue with the tossing of the grenade. Meanwhile, during this time when the server confirmed that the client could throw that grenade, the client started playing through the animation sequence that it does when a player throws a grenade. If this is left unchecked (that is, the server doesn't respond back in time), the player will finish swinging his arm forward, but nothing will be thrown, which, in this context, will look like a normal action [*Aldridge, David (2011), I Shot You First: Networking the Gameplay of HALO: REACH. GDC 2011*].

How close is close enough?

Another use case is that a client has the current state of the game along with the player's input information. The player runs the next turn's simulation and renders the snake at a certain position. A few frames later, the server tells the client that the snake is actually at a different position now. How do we fix this?

In situations where we need to change a player's position, it might look strange if the player launches a blue robot into the air and over a pit with spikes at the bottom, and a few frames later (after the server syncs up all of the clients), we suddenly see the robot several pixels away from where the player expected it to be. However, then again, there are cases where the adjustment needed from an update from the server is small enough so that simply teleporting the player from point A to point B is not noticeable. This would be heavily dependent on the type of game and the individual situation.

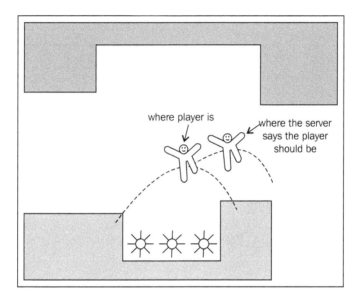

For the purpose of our Snake game, we can choose to teleport if we determine that the discrepancy between our prediction of where the snake should be, and where the server tells us the snake is, is only off by one unit in either (not both) axis, except if the head is off by one unit in both the axes but adjusting one of the axis would put us at the neck of the snake. This way, the player would only see the snake change the position of its head by one place.

For example, if our prediction puts the player's head at point (8,15), and the snake is moving from right to left, but the server's update shows that it should be at point (7,16), we would not teleport to the new point because that would require adjusting two axes.

However, if we still have the snake moving to the left and its head is now at point (8,15), and the server update puts it at point (7,15), (8,14), (8,16), (9,15), (9,14), or (9,16), we can simply teleport the head to the new point, and in the next update, the rest of the body of the snake would be repositioned, as needed.

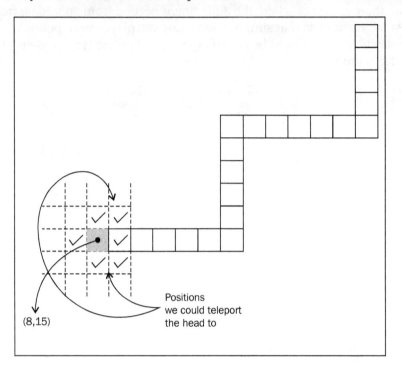

Positions we could teleport the head to

(8,15)

```
// ch4/snake-ch4/share/snake.js

Snake.prototype.sync = function(serverState) {
    var diffX = serverState.head.x - this.head.x;
    var diffY = serverState.head.y - this.head.y;

    if (diffX === 0 && diffY === 0) {
        this.inSync = true;
        return true;
    }

    this.inSync = false;

    // Teleport to new position if:
    //    - Off by one in one of the axis
```

```
//    - Off by one in both axes, but only one unit from the neck
if ((diffX === 0 && diffY === 1)
        || (diffX === 1 && diffY === 0)
        || (this.pieces[0].x === serverState.head.x && diffY === 1)
        || (this.pieces[0].y === serverState.head.y && diffX === 1)
    ){

    this.head.x = serverState.head.x;
    this.head.y = serverState.head.y;

    this.inSync = false;
    return true;
}

// TODO: Implement interpolation error correction strategy here

return false;
};
```

You will notice that teleporting could put the head of the snake over itself, which, under normal circumstances, would result in the player losing the game. However, when this happens, the game won't check for that collision again until the next frame is updated. At this point, the head will be first moved forward, which will readjust the rest of the body of the snake and thus remove any possible collisions.

Smooth user experience

Another way to adjust between the player's current position and the position set by the server is to gradually and smoothly move towards that point through the course of multiple frames. In other words, we interpolate between our current position and the position we want to get to.

The way interpolation works is simple, as explained here:

1. First determine how many frames you want the interpolation to take.
2. Then determine how many units you will need to move in each direction per frame.
3. Finally, move each frame a little bit until you get to the destination point in the desired amount of frames.

Essentially, we simply move a percentage of the way towards the target point at the same percentage of the time we wish to get there. In other words, if we would like to get to the target position in 10 frames, then at each frame we move 10 percent of the total distance. Thus, we can abstract away the following formula:

$a = (1 - t) * b + t * c$

Here, t is a number between zero and one, which represents a percentage value between 0 percent and 100 percent (this is the current distance between the starting point and the target point).

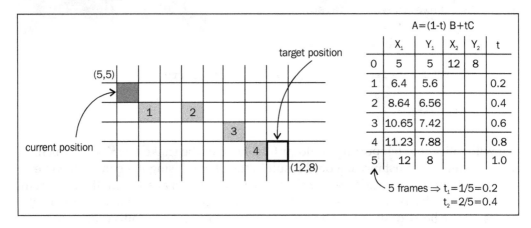

We can implement the linear interpolation method in the snake class directly; however, the obsessed object-oriented designer inside of you might argue that this mathematical procedure might be better suited inside an entirely separate utility class that is imported and used by the snake class.

```
// ch4/snake-ch4/share/snake.js

Snake.prototype.interpolate = function(currFrame, src, dest,
totalFrames) {
    var t = currFrame / totalFrames;

    return (1 - t) * src + dest * totalFrames ;
};
```

This interpolation method will take (besides the source and destination points) the current frame within the animation as well as the total number of frames that the animation will last. As a result, we'll need some way to keep track of the current frame and reset it to zero when we wish to start the animation again.

A good place to reset the interpolation sequence is in the `socket` callback, which is where we first learn that we might need to interpolate towards a different position.

```
// ch4/snake-ch4/share/app.client.js

socket.on(gameEvents.client_playerState, function(data){
    otherPlayers = data.filter(function(_player){

        if (_player.id == player.id) {
            serverState = _player;
            serverState.currFrame = 0;

            return false;
        }

        return true;
    });
});
```

We will then also need to update the `snake` class so that we can configure the maximum amount of frames that each interpolation cycle can handle.

```
// ch4/snake-ch4/share/snake.js

var Snake = function (id, x, y, color_hex, width, height,
interpMaxFrames) {
    this.id = id;
    this.color = color_hex;
    this.head = {x: x, y: y};
    this.pieces = [this.head];
    this.width = width || 16;
    this.height = height || 16;
    this.interpMaxFrames = interpMaxFrames || 3;
    this.readyToGrow = false;
    this.input = {};
    this.inSync = true;
};
```

With this in place, we can now implement linear interpolation in our `sync` method so that the snake can interpolate smoothly to its actual position over the course of a few frames. The number of frames that you choose to arrive at the target destination can be dynamically set depending on the distance to travel, or you can leave it constant as per your game's individual case.

```
// ch4/snake-ch4/share/snake.js

Snake.prototype.sync = function(serverState) {
```

```
    var diffX = serverState.head.x - this.head.x;
    var diffY = serverState.head.y - this.head.y;

    if (diffX === 0 && diffY === 0) {
        this.inSync = true;

        return true;
    }

    this.inSync = false;

    // Teleport to new position if:
    //   - Off by one in one of the axis
    //   - Off by one in both axes, but only one unit from the
neck
    if ((diffX === 0 && diffY === 1) ||
        (diffX === 1 && diffY === 0) ||
        (this.pieces[0].x === serverState.head.x && diffY === 1)
||
        (this.pieces[0].y === serverState.head.y && diffX === 1))
{

        this.head.x = serverState.head.x;
        this.head.y = serverState.head.y;

        this.inSync = true;

        return true;
    }

    // Interpolate towards correct point until close enough to
teleport
    if (serverState.currFrame < this.interpMaxFrames) {
        this.head.x = this.interpolate(
            serverState.currFrame,
            this.head.x,
            serverState.head.x,
            this.interpMaxFrames
        );
        this.head.y = this.interpolate(
            serverState.currFrame,
            this.head.y,
            serverState.head.y,
            this.interpMaxFrames
```

```
            );
    }

    return false;
};
```

Finally, you will notice that, in this current implementation of our client-server setup, the client receives the exact positions of the other players, so no prediction is made about them. Thus, their positions are always in sync with the server and need no error corrections or interpolations.

Summary

The focus of this chapter was to reduce the perceived latency between the authoritative server and the clients that it runs. We saw how client prediction can be used to give the player immediate feedback while the server determines the validity of a player's requested move and intent. We then looked at how to incorporate the lockstep method on the server so that all the clients are updated together, and every client can also deterministically reproduce the same world state that is calculated by the game server.

Finally, we looked at the two ways to correct a bad client prediction. The methods we implemented are teleportation and linear interpolation. Using these two error-correction methods allows us to show the player a close approximation of what should happen as a result of his or her input, but it also makes sure that their multiplayer experience is accurate and identical to what other players are experiencing.

In the next chapter, we will take a step into the future and play with some of the newer HTML5 APIs, including the Gamepad API, which will allow us to ditch the keyboard and use the more traditional game pad to control our games, Full-screen mode API, and WebRTC, which will allow us to do true peer-to-peer gaming and skip the client-server model for a while, and much more.

5
Leveraging the Bleeding Edge

So far in the book, we have focused our discussion on topics related to multiplayer game development. This time around, with the exception of **WebRTC**, we will discuss some of the newest APIs in HTML5 that, by themselves, have very little to do with multiplayer gaming, but they afford great opportunities in the context of game development.

In this chapter, we will discuss the following principles and concepts:

- Connecting peers directly with WebRTC
- Adding game pads to your browser-based games
- Maximizing your games in the **fullscreen** mode
- Accessing the user's media devices

HTML5 – the final frontier

Although the technologies with which we'll be experimenting in this chapter are exciting and very promising, we must not as yet get too attached to any one of them. At the very least, we must be cautious about how we use these APIs because they are still either experimental, or the specification is either in the Working Draft or Candidate Recommendation stage. In other words, chances are pretty good that, as of this writing and for the near, foreseeable future after the publication of this book, browser support for each feature may vary, APIs that do support each feature might differ slightly across browsers, and the future of the APIs may be uncertain.

The **World Wide Web Consortium (W3C)** defines four development stages (also known as maturity levels) that every specification evolves through before the specification is final, stable, and considered to be of the W3C standard. These four stages are **Working Draft**, **Candidate Recommendation**, **Proposed Recommendation**, and **W3C Recommendation**.

The initial level is Working Draft, in which the community discusses the proposed specification and defines the precise details that they try to accomplish. At this level, the recommendation is very unstable, and its eventual publication is all but guaranteed.

The next one is the Candidate Recommendation level, in which feedback is elicited from groups that implement the recommendation. Here, the standard is still unstable and subject to change (or deprecation, as is sometimes the case), but it tends to change less frequently than when it is at the Working Draft stage.

Once a specification document is published as a Proposed Recommendation, the advisory committee at W3C reviews the proposal. If at least four weeks have gone by since the review period began and the document has received enough endorsement from the community and implementers, the document is forwarded for publication as a recommendation.

Finally, when a specification becomes a W3C Recommendation, it carries with it the stamp of approval from W3C as an endorsed standard. Sadly, even at this point, there are no guarantees that a browser will support a standard or implement it according to the specification. However, in our day and age, all major browsers do a pretty good job of following specifications and implementing all the useful standards that are out there.

Maximizing your game with the fullscreen mode

Of all the APIs that we'll discuss in this chapter, fullscreen is the simplest to understand and use. As you might have guessed, what this API allows you to do is set an HTML element node that can be presented in the fullscreen mode.

Note that, although the first Editor's Draft (the maturation level that comes before a recommended standard becomes a Working Draft) for the fullscreen mode was published in October 2011, the specification is still in its early drafting stages. (refer to the following article for more information: *Using fullscreen mode, (July 2014)*. `https://developer.mozilla.org/en-US/docs/Web/Guide/API/DOM/Using_full_screen_mode`).

As for the current browser support, you will find that it is pretty safe to use the API in all modern browsers, although today there are subtle differences in implementation as well as how you should enable the fullscreen mode.

The main thing to keep in mind when using fullscreen is that you must set a single element to the fullscreen mode. This element can indeed have a subtree of element nodes, but you will still need to enable the fullscreen mode on a particular element. In the context of game development, you will most likely set the main canvas element to fullscreen, but this is not a hard requirement. You could just as well request that the browser make the entire document fullscreen by calling the `requetFullscreen()` method on the body element.

There are two methods that are involved in setting an element in the fullscreen mode, and removing an element from the fullscreen mode. The methods are `requestFullscreen` and `exitFullscreen` respectively. Note that as of this writing, all major browsers implement these methods under their individual vendor prefix.

In addition, remember that the fullscreen mode cannot be enabled unless a user-initiated event makes the request to the browser. In other words, you cannot simply attempt to change the body element to fullscreen as soon as your DOM has loaded. Likewise, you cannot programmatically fire a DOM event (such as triggering a fake click on the page or using JavaScript to scroll the page, thus firing an `onScroll` event) and use the event handler callback to trick the browser into thinking that it was the user that initiated the action.

```
<!doctype html>
<html>
<head>
    <title> Fullscreen</title>
    <!-- [some custom CSS here, left out for brevity] -->
</head>
<body>
<ul>
    <li>
        <span>1</span>
    </li>
    <li>
        <span>0</span>
    </li>
    <li>
        <span>0</span>
    </li>
    <li>
        <span>1</span>
    </li>
```

```
    </ul>
    <script>
        var list = document.querySelector('ul');

        list.addEventListener('click', function (event) {
            var block = event.target;
            block.requestFullscreen();
        });
    </script>
    </body>
    </html>
```

The preceding code demonstrates how to set an element to the fullscreen mode after that element receives a click. In this case, you may have noticed that we assume that whatever browser executes that code will have dropped their vendor support, and we can simply call requestFullscreen() as it was intended.

A better way to go about this today, since browsers have not yet implemented the specification without a vendor prefixing the API, is to use a polyfill or helper function that detects whether a vendor prefix is needed and does what is needed to make it work.

```
var reqFullscreen = (function () {
    var method = (function () {
        var el = document.createElement('div');
        var supported = '';
        var variations = [
            'requestFullscreen',
            'msRequestFullscreen',
            'mozRequestFullScreen',
            'webkitRequestFullscreen'
        ];

        variations.some(function (method) {
            supported = method;
            return el[method] instanceof Function;
        });

        return supported;
    }());

    return function (element) {
        element[method]();
    };
}());
```

```
var list = document.querySelector('ul');

list.addEventListener('click', function (event) {
    var block = event.target;
    reqFullscreen(block);
});
```

The preceding sample code creates a function called reqFullscreen, which does the heavy lifting for us by determining if a vendor prefix is needed; it then remembers which version of the fullscreen request needs to be made. We then call that function when we want the element to go the fullscreen mode, by passing it within the element.

> It seems that the makers of browsers have the goal to make experimental APIs as confusing as possible for end users. In the case of fullscreen, note that the specification names the interface functions as requestFullscreen and exitFullscreen (where the word Fullscreen only capitalizes the first letter).
>
> Every vendor prefix, except for Mozilla Firefox, follows the specification with regards to the function names—that is, webkitRequestFullscreen and msRequestFullscreen. Mozilla Firefox differs because it implements mozRequestFullScreen, which differs from the other vendors since it spells FullScreen as two words in the camel case. As a final detail, the folks at Webkit decided to please both the sides of the crowd by implementing both the versions: webkitRequestFullscreen and webkitRequestFullScreen.

In the previous image, our page is not in the the fullscreen mode. However, when you click on one of the elements, that element is presented in the fullscreen mode:

You may observe that the only requirement that the browser imposes is that a user action must initiate the request to enable fullscreen. This does not mean that the action must be on the same element that is set to fullscreen, as shown in the following example:

```
var list = document.querySelector('ul');
var btn = document.querySelector('button');

btn.addEventListener('click', function (event) {
    // Somehow determine what element to use
    var firstBlock = list.children[0].children[0];

    reqFullscreen(firstBlock);
});
```

The preceding example binds to a button element. then add a click handler that sets some other element to enable in fullscreen mode.

We can check whether a specific element is in the fullscreen mode by looking up an automatically updated property of the document object.

```
var element = document.webkitFullscreenElement;
```

When you run the previous statement, it will return a reference to any element that's currently in the fullscreen mode; otherwise, it will return a null value.

We can also query the document to test whether the document can be enabled as fullscreen.

```
var canFullscreen = document.webkitFullscreenEnabled; // => bool
```

Finally, there is a special CSS pseudo selector that allows us to target the element in fullscreen. Again, this selector is also vendor prefixed as of this moment.

```
full-screen,
:-moz-full-screen,
:-moz-full-screen-ancestor,
:-webkit-full-screen {
    font-size: 50vw;
    line-height: 1.25;
    /* … */
}
```

Note that the selector targets the very element that called `requestFullscreen`. In the preceding example, the styles specified before apply to the **ul li span**.

Better controlling with gamepad

Over the last several years, we have seen a very welcome and robust list of new APIs added to HTML5. These include WebSockets, canvas, local storage, WebGL, and many more. In the context of game development, the next natural step was to add standard support for a gamepad.

Similar to the fullscreen mode, the gamepad API is still in the very early drafting stages. In fact, gamepad support is even more "primitive" than fullscreen. Although you will find browser support to be adequate, working with the API can be buggy and somewhat unpredictable. However, the gamepad API does provide a good enough interface for a great end user experience. As the specification matures, the prospect of adding a gamepad to the browser is very exciting and promising.

The first thing you'll notice about the gamepad API is the way in which it differs from all other input APIs in the DOM as it is not driven by events such as a mouse or keyboard. For example, although every input with a keyboard triggers an event (in other words, a registered callback is invoked), input from a connected gamepad can only be detected by manually polling the hardware. In other words, the browser will fire gamepad-related events to let you know that a gamepad has connected and disconnected. However, beyond these kinds of events, the browser does not fire an event every time a key is pressed on a connected gamepad.

To start using a gamepad in your game, you will first need to wait for one to connect to the game. This is done by registering a callback to listen to the global gamepadconnected event:

```
/**
 * @type {GamepadEvent} event
 */
function onGamepadConnected(event) {
    var gamepad = event.gamepad;
}

window.addEventListener('gamepadconnected', onGamepadConnected);
```

The gamepadconnected event will fire any time a gamepad is connected to your computer during the lifetime of your game. If a gamepad is already connected before the script loads, the gamepadconnected event will not fire until the player presses a button on the gamepad. While this may seem weird at first, this restriction was put in place for a very good reason — namely, to protect the player from being fingerprinted by ill-intentioned scripts. However, requiring the user to press a button before the controller is activated is not that big of a deal since the player will need to press a button at some point if he or she wishes to play your game. The only drawback to this, as you can imagine, is that we won't know right off the bat whether the user has a gamepad connected to the computer yet. Still, coming up with creative solutions to work around this limitation is not too difficult of a task.

The GamepadEvent object exposes a gamepad property, which is a reference to the actual Gamepad object, which is what we're after. The interesting thing about this object is that it is not self updating like other objects in JavaScript. In other words, whenever the browser receives input from a connected gamepad, it keeps track of its state internally. Then, once you poll the gamepad state, the browser creates a new Gamepad object with all the updated properties to reflect the current state of the controller.

```
function update(){
    var gamepads = navigator.getGamepads();
    var gp_1 = gamepads[0];

    if (gp_1.buttons[1].pressed) {
        // Button 1 pressed on first connected gamepad
    }

    if (gp_1.axes[1] < 0) {
        // Left stick held to the left on first connected gamepad
```

```
        }

        requestAnimationFrame(update);
    }
```

During each `update` cycle, you will need to obtain the most recent snapshot of the gamepad object and look up its state.

The `Gamepad` object interface defines no methods, but its several properties are as follows:

```
interface Gamepad {
    readonly attribute DOMString id;
    readonly attribute long index;
    readonly attribute boolean connected;
    readonly attribute DOMHighResTimeStamp timestamp;
    readonly attribute GamepadMappingType mapping;
    readonly attribute double[] axes;
    readonly attribute GamepadButton[] buttons;
};
```

The `id` attribute describes the actual hardware connected to the application. If you connect a gamepad through some USB adapter, it is likely that the `id` will reference the adapter device rather than the actual controller that was used.

The `index` will reference the `Gamepad` object within the `GamepadList` object, which is what the browser provides in response to `navigator.getGamepads()`. Using this index value, we can get a reference to a specific gamepad that we wish to query.

As expected, the `boolean connected` property indicates whether a particular gamepad is still connected to the application. If a gamepad disconnects prior to a call to `navigator.getGamepads()`, the corresponding element that is based on a `Gamepad.index` offset will be null in the `GamepadList`. However, if a reference to a `Gamepad` object is obtained, but the hardware disconnects, the object will still have its connected property set to true because those properties are not dynamically updated. In summary, this property is superfluous and will probably be removed from the spec in future updates.

We can check when the browser last updated the `gamepad` state by looking at the `timestamp` attribute on a `Gamepad` object.

A particularly interesting attribute is `mapping`. The idea behind this is that there can be several standard mappings so as to make it easier to wire up the application corresponding to the way the hardware is laid out.

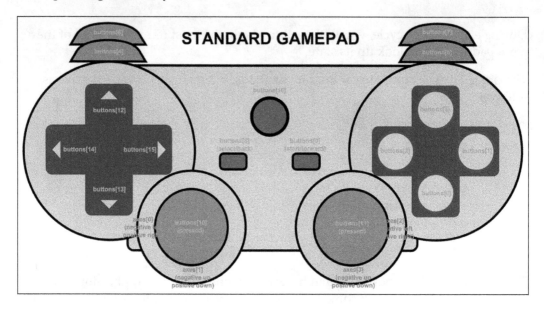

Currently, there is only one standard mapping, which can be identified by the name `standard`, as demonstrated previously (for more information refer to, *Gamepad W3C Working Draft 29 April 2015.* `http://www.w3.org/TR/gamepad`). If the browser doesn't know how to layout the controller, it will respond with an empty string for the `mapping` attribute and map the buttons and axes in the best way that it can. In such cases, the application should probably ask the user to manually map the buttons that the application uses. Keep in mind that there are cases where the d-pad buttons are mapped to one of the axes, so handle each case with care:

```
var btns = {
        arrow_up: document.querySelector('.btn .arrow-up'),
        arrow_down: document.querySelector('.btn .arrow-down'),
        arrow_left: document.querySelector('.btn .arrow-left'),
        arrow_right: document.querySelector('.btn .arrow-right'),

        button_a: document.querySelector('.buttons .btn-y'),
        button_b: document.querySelector('.buttons .btn-x'),
        button_x: document.querySelector('.buttons .btn-b'),
        button_y: document.querySelector('.buttons .btn-a'),

        button_select: document.querySelector('.controls .btn-
select'),
```

```
        button_start: document.querySelector('.controls .btn-
start'),

        keyCodes: {
            37: 'arrow_left',
            38: 'arrow_up',
            39: 'arrow_right',
            40: 'arrow_down',

            32: 'button_a',
            65: 'button_b',
            68: 'button_x',
            83: 'button_y',

            27: 'button_select',
            16: 'button_start'
        },

        keyNames: {
            axe_left: 0,
            axe_left_val: -1,

            axe_right: 0,
            axe_right_val: 1,

            axe_up: 1,
            axe_up_val: -1,

            axe_down: 1,
            axe_down_val: 1
        }
    };

    Object.keys(btns.keyCodes).map(function(index){
        btns.keyNames[btns.keyCodes[index]] = index;
    });

function displayKey(keyCode, pressed) {
    var classAction = pressed ? 'add' : 'remove';

    if (btns.keyCodes[keyCode]) {
        btns[btns.keyCodes[keyCode]].classList[classAction]('active');
    }
}
```

```
function update(now) {
        requestAnimationFrame(update);

        // GamepadList[0] references the first gamepad that
connected to the app
        gamepad = navigator.getGamepads().item(0);

        if (gamepad.buttons[0].pressed) {
            displayKey(btns.keyNames.button_x, true);
        } else {
            displayKey(btns.keyNames.button_x, false);
        }

        if (gamepad.buttons[1].pressed) {
            displayKey(btns.keyNames.button_a, true);
        } else {
            displayKey(btns.keyNames.button_a, false);
        }

        if (gamepad.buttons[2].pressed) {
            displayKey(btns.keyNames.button_b, true);
        } else {
            displayKey(btns.keyNames.button_b, false);
        }

        if (gamepad.buttons[3].pressed) {
            displayKey(btns.keyNames.button_y, true);
        } else {
            displayKey(btns.keyNames.button_y, false);
        }

        if (gamepad.buttons[8].pressed) {
            displayKey(btns.keyNames.button_select, true);
        } else {
            displayKey(btns.keyNames.button_select, false);
        }

        if (gamepad.buttons[9].pressed) {
            displayKey(btns.keyNames.button_start, true);
        } else {
            displayKey(btns.keyNames.button_start, false);
        }

        if (gamepad.axes[btns.keyNames.axe_left] ===
btns.keyNames.axe_left_val){
            displayKey(btns.keyNames.arrow_left, true);
        } else {
            displayKey(btns.keyNames.arrow_left, false);
        }
```

```
        if (gamepad.axes[btns.keyNames.axe_down] ===
btns.keyNames.axe_down_val) {
            displayKey(btns.keyNames.arrow_down, true);
        } else {
            displayKey(btns.keyNames.arrow_down, false);
        }

        if (gamepad.axes[btns.keyNames.axe_up] ===
btns.keyNames.axe_up_val) {
            displayKey(btns.keyNames.arrow_up, true);
        } else {
            displayKey(btns.keyNames.arrow_up, false);
        }

        if (gamepad.axes[btns.keyNames.axe_right] ===
btns.keyNames.axe_right_val) {
            displayKey(btns.keyNames.arrow_right, true);
        } else {
            displayKey(btns.keyNames.arrow_right, false);
        }
    }

    window.addEventListener('gamepadconnected', function (e) {
        update(0);
    });
```

The preceding example connects a gamepad with no recognizable mapping; thus, it assigns each button to a specific layout. Since the d-pad buttons map to the left axis in this particular case, we check for that state when we want to determine whether the d-pad is being used. The output of this demonstration can be seen as follows:

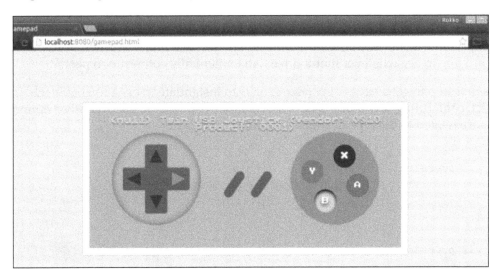

Often, you might wish to offer the user the ability to choose the way they would prefer to interact with your game—using a keyboard and mouse, a gamepad, or both. In the previous example, this is precisely the reason why the `btns` object referenced seemingly random and arbitrary `keyCode` values. These values are mapped to specific keyboard keys so that the player could use the arrow keys on a standard keyboard or a gamepad.

Peer-to-peer with WebRTC

One of the most exciting APIs to come out in recent years is WebRTC (which stand for Web real-time communication). The purpose of this API is to allow users to communicate in real-time streaming audio and video across platforms that support the technology.

WebRTC is made up of several individual APIs and can be broken down into three separate components, namely `getUserMedia` (which we'll discuss in more depth in the next section), `RTCPeerConnection`, and `RTCDataChannel`.

Since we'll discuss `getUserMedia` in the next section, we'll leave a more involved definition for it when we get there (although the name might give away what the API is intended to do).

`RTCPeerConnection` is what we use to connect two peers together. Once a connection has been established, we can use `RTCDataChannel` and transmit any data (including binary data) between the peers. In the context of game development, we can use `RTCDataChannel` to send a player's state to each peer without the need for a server linking each player.

To get started with `RTCPeerConnection`, we need some way to tell each peer about the other one. Note that the WebRTC specification deliberately leaves out any specific way in which this data transfer should take place. In other words, we are free to use whatever method we like to manually connect two peers.

The first step to get a `RTCPeerConnection` is to instantiate `RTCPeerConnection` object, configuring it with the **STUN** servers that you wish to use and other options that are related to the type of connection that you expect:

```
var pcConfig = {
    iceServers: [{
        url: 'stun:stun.1.google.com:19302'
    }]
};

var pcOptions = {
```

```
    optional: [{
        RtpDataChannels: true
    }]
};

var pc = new webkitRTCPeerConnection(pcConfig, pcOptions);
```

Here, we use a public STUN server that Google provides free of cost. We also use a vendor prefix to be consistent with the other examples in this chapter. As of this writing, every vendor that implements WebRTC in some fashion uses a vendor prefix.

If you're not too familiar with STUN, **Interactive Connectivity Establishment (ICE)**, **NAT**, **TURN**, and **SDP**, don't worry too much about it. While this book won't explain these networking concepts in any depth, you won't really need to know too much about them in order to follow the examples in this chapter and to implement data channels in your own game.

In brief, a STUN server is used to tell a client about its public IP address and whether the client is behind a router's NAT, so another peer can connect to it. Thus, we use one in creating our RTCPeerConnection.

Again, with simplicity and brevity in mind, an ICE candidate allows the browser the reach another browser directly.

Once we have an RTCPeerConnection ready, we connect to a peer by offering to connect with them. The first step is to create an offer, which describes how the other client would connect back to us. Here is where we use a protocol of our choosing to inform the other peer about our offer. Commonly, this would be done using a WebSocket, but in order to demonstrate each step more explicitly, we will use the oldest communication protocol known to man: **mouth to mouth**:

```
/**
 *
 */
function makeMessage(msg, user, color) {
    var container = document.createElement('p');
    var tag = document.createElement('span');
    var text = document.createElement('span');

    if (color) {
        tag.classList.add(color);
    } else if (nickColor) {
        tag.classList.add(nickColor);
```

```
        }

        tag.textContent = '[' + (user || nick) + '] ';
        text.textContent = msg;

        container.appendChild(tag);
        container.appendChild(text);

        var out = document.getElementById('out');
        var footer = document.getElementById('outFooter');
        out.appendChild(container);
        footer.scrollIntoView();
    }

    /**
     *
     */
    function createOffer() {
        pc.createOffer(function (offer) {
            // Note #1
            makeMessage('offer: ' + encodeURIComponent(offer.sdp));

            // Note #2
            pc.setLocalDescription(new RTCSessionDescription(offer),
                // Note #3
                function () {},

                // Note #4
                function (e) {
                    console.error(e);
                    makeMessage('error creating offer');
                }
            );
        });
    }
```

In this *hello world* demonstration of WebRTC's peer-to-peer connection, we'll build a simple chat room with no servers in the middle (except for the STUN server that we need to initiate the peer-to-peer connection).

Given the preceding sample code, we can assume some HTML structure with an input element where we can enter text and commands and use them to drive the WebRTC components.

The previous screenshot shows the output once we invoke the createOffer function shown previously. We'll make extensive use of the makeMessage function to help us see messages initiated by the system (meaning the WebRTC API) as well as messages from the other peer with whom we're trying to connect and chat.

Note #1 in the previous code sample is intended to draw your attention to the way we' display the offer's **Session Description Protocol** (**SDP**), which is a protocol for *negotiating session capabilities between the peers* (taken from Suhas Nandakumar article on, *SDP for the WebRTC*, http://tools.ietf.org/id/draft-nandakumar-rtcweb-sdp-01.html). Since line breaks are meaningful in the protocol, we need to preserve every character in that string. By encoding the string, we guarantee that the string provided to us by the framework is not altered in any way (although it makes it slightly less readable for us humans).

Note #2 shows the second step of this information exchange process that will connect us to another peer. Here, we need to set our own client's session description. You can think of this as you remembering your own home address (or PO box, if you're into engaging in a series of letter communications with a pen pal).

Note #3 and Note #4 are the second and third arguments that we send to the RTCSessionDescription constructor. They are the success and error callback functions respectively, which we are not very concerned with at the moment. Actually, we do care about the error callback function because we wish to be informed about any possible error that might occur when we attempt to reach the STUN server, and so on.

Now that we have an `offer` object, we just need to let the other peer know what that offer looks like. The two things that make up the offer are the SDP block and the type of session description.

Once our peer knows what the SDP block looks like, he or she can instantiate an `RTCSessionDescription` object and set the SDP and type properties. Next, the second peer sets that session description as his or her own remote session descriptor. In this case, we just open a new window to represent the second peer and transmit the SDP string via the ever-so-sophisticated *copy + paste* method.

```
function setRemoteDesc(sdp, type) {
    var offer = new RTCSessionDescription();
    offer.sdp = decodeURIComponent(sdp);
    offer.type = type;

    makeMessage('remote desc: ' + offer.sdp);

    pc.setRemoteDescription(new RTCSessionDescription(offer),
        function () {
        },
        function (e) {
            console.log(e);
            makeMessage('error setting remote desc');
        }
    );
}
```

Here, we manually create an `offer` object for the other client. We use the SDP data that we obtained from the first client and set the second client's session description type to `offer`. This offer is set to the second client's remote descriptor. You can think of this, in the example of you writing to a pen pal, as the pen pal writing down your home address so that he or she knows where to send their letters.

After the second peer has made note of your session description, the next step is for that offer to be accepted. In RTC lingo, the second peer needs to answer to this offer. Similar to how we called `createOffer()` to create the initial offer, we call `createAnswer()` on the `webkitRTCPeerConnection` object. The output of this call is also a session description object, except that it contains the second user's SDP, and the session description type is `answer` instead of `offer`.

```
function answerOffer() {
    pc.createAnswer(function (answer) {
        makeMessage('answer: ' + encodeURIComponent(answer.sdp));
        pc.setLocalDescription(new RTCSessionDescription(answer));
    }, function (e) {
```

```
        console.log(e);
        makeMessage('error creating answer');
    });
}
```

Here, the remote peer first sets its own local description from the SDP that it received from the `answer` object. Then, we display that to the screen so that we can use that same information as the first peer's (the `local peer`) remote description. This is representative of your pen pal first remembering their own home address and then letting you have a copy of it so that you now know where to send your letters.

Now that both peers know where the other can be reached, all that is needed is a way to reach the other peer. This level of detail is abstracted away from the data channel. So, before we can use the data channel, we need to add at least one ICE candidate to the peer connection object.

When each peer creates their `offer` and `answer` object, the peer connection object receives one or more ICE candidate references. In this demo, we print these out to the screen when we receive them, so that at this point we can copy and paste the data that makes up each ICE candidate, and thus we can recreate them on the opposing peer's machine, and add the ICE candidate to the peer connection object.

```
pc.onicecandidate = function (event) {
    if (event.candidate) {
        makeMessage('ice candidate: ' + JSON.stringify(event.
candidate), 'sys', 'sys');
    }
};

function addIceCandidate(candidate) {
    pc.addIceCandidate(candidate);
}

addIceCandidate(JSON.parse({
    /* encoded candidate object from onIceCandidate callback */
}));
```

Once each peer has the other peer's session descriptor and there is an ICE candidate to guide the browser to the other peer, we can start sending messages directly from one to the other.

The next step is to simply send and receive messages using the `DataChannel` object. Here, the API is very similar to WebSocket's API, where we call a `send()` method on the channel object to send data to the peer, and we register a `onmessage` event handler from which we receive data from the other side of the peer-to-peer connection. The main difference here is that, unlike the WebSocket scenario, we're now connected directly to the other peer, so sending a message is blazingly fast:

```javascript
// When creating the RTCPeerConnection object, we also create the
DataChannel
var pc = new webkitRTCPeerConnection(pcConfig, pcOptions);
var channelName = 'packtRtc';
var dc = dc = pc.createDataChannel(channelName);

function sendMessage(msg) {
    if (dc.readyState === 'open') {
        var data = {
            msg: msg,
            user: nick,
            color: nickColor
        };

        // Since this is a chat app, we want to see our own message
        makeMessage(msg);

        // The actual send command
        dc.send(JSON.stringify(data));
    } else {
        makeMessage('Could not send message: DataChannel not yet
open.');
    }
}

dc.onmessage = function (event) {
    var data = JSON.parse(event.data);
    makeMessage(data.msg, data.user, data.color);
};

dc.onopen = function () {
    makeMessage('dataChannel open', 'sys', 'sys');
};

dc.onerror = function (e) {
    makeMessage('dataChannel error: ' + e, 'sys', 'sys');
};
```

```
dc.onclose = function () {
    makeMessage('dataChannel close', 'sys', 'sys');
};
```

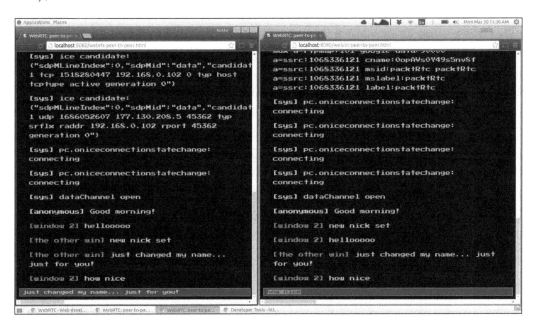

To summarize, before we can start using our `DataChannel` to communicate with the other peer, we need to manually (meaning, outside the real of WebRTC APIs) configure each peer relative to each other. Often, you will want to first connect the peers through a WebSocket and use that connection to create and answer the offer from the initiating peer. In addition, data sent through the `DataChannel` is not limited to text only. We can send binary data, such as video and audio using another WebRTC API, which we'll discuss in the next section.

Capturing the moment with Media Capture

One of the newer components of online multiplayer games is the social aspect that involves real-time voice and video communication. This last component can be perfectly satisfied by using HTML **Media Capture** APIs, which allow you to access your player's camera and microphone. Once you have gained access to a camera and microphone, you can broadcast that data to other players, save them as audio and video files, or even create a standalone experience that is based on that alone.

The *hello world* example of Media Capture is probably the eye candy of audio visualization demonstration. We can achieve this with a mixture of Media Capture and **Web Audio** API. With media capture, we can actually receive the raw audio data from the user's microphone; then, we can use Web Audio to connect the data and analyze it. With that data in place, we can lean on the canvas API to render the data representing the sound waves that was received by the microphone.

First, let us take a more involved look at Media Capture. Then, we'll look at the important pieces of Web Audio and leave it as an exercise for you to find a better, more complete, and dedicated source to deepen your' understanding of the rest of the Web Audio API.

Currently, media capture is in candidate recommendation, so we still need to look for and include vendor prefixes. For brevity, we will assume **Webkit targetting** (*HTML Media Capture W3C Candidate Recommendation*, (September 2014). `http://www.w3.org/TR/html-media-capture/`).

We begin by calling the `getUserMedia` function on the navigator object. (for more information about the `window.navigator` property, go to `https://developer.mozilla.org/en-US/docs/Web/API/Window/navigator`.) In this, we specify any constraints about the media we wish to capture, such as the audio, the video frame rate that we want, and so on:

```
var constraints = {
    audio: false,
    video: {
        mandatory: {
            minAspectRatio: 1.333,
            maxAspectRatio: 1.334
        },
        optional: {
            width: {
                min: 640,
                max: 1920,
                ideal: 1280
            },
            height: {
                min: 480,
                max: 1080,
                ideal: 720
            },
            framerate: 30
        }
    }
};

var allowCallback = function(stream){
    // use captured local media stream
```

```
    // ...
};

var denyCallback = function(e){
    // user denied permission to let your app access media devices
    console.error('Could not access media devices', e);
};

navigator.webkitGetUserMedia(constraints, allowCallback,
denyCallback);
```

In its simplest form, the constraints dictionary only includes a key indicating the type of media that we wish to capture, followed by a `Boolean` value that represents our intent. Optionally, any false values can be shorthanded by leaving out the attribute altogether.

```
var  constraints = {
    audio: true,
    video: false
};

// the above is equivalent to simply {audio: true}

navigator.webkitGetUserMedia(constraints, allowCallback,
denyCallback);
```

Once the call to `getUserMedia` is executed, the browser will display a warning message to the user, alerting him or her that the page is attempting to access media devices; this will give the user a chance to allow or deny such a request:

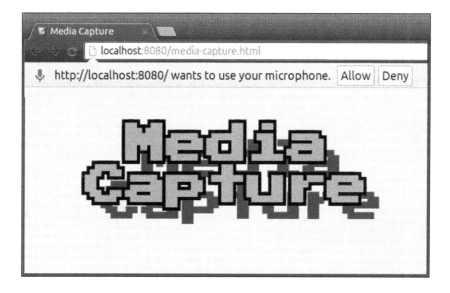

Although it is different from the old `window.alert`, `window.confirm`, and `window.prompt` APIs, the browser-generated prompt is always asynchronous and non-blocking. This is the reason for providing callback functions for the cases where the user allows or denies your request.

Once we have been granted access to the user's audio device, as in the previous example, we can leverage the Web Audio API and create an `AudioContext` object; from this, we can then create a media stream source:

```
var allowCallback = function(stream) {
    var audioContext = new AudioContext();
    var mic = audioContext.createMediaStreamSource(stream);

    // ...
};
```

As you may have guessed, a `MediaStream` object represents the microphone as a source of data. With that reference, we can now connect the microphone to an `AnalyserNode` to help us break down the audio input into something that we can represent visually:

```
var allowCallback = function(stream) {
    var audioContext = new AudioContext();
    var mic = audioContext.createMediaStreamSource(stream);

    var analyser = audioContext.createAnalyser();
    analyser.smoothingTimeConstant = 0.3;
    analyser.fftSize = 128;

    mic.connect(analyser);

    // ...
};
```

The next step is to use the `analyser` object and get the frequency data from the audio source. With this on hand, we can just render it to some existing canvas as we see fit:

```
var allowCallback = function(stream) {
    var audioContext = new AudioContext();
    var mic = audioContext.createMediaStreamSource(stream);

    var analyser = audioContext.createAnalyser();
    analyser.smoothingTimeConstant = 0.3;
    analyser.fftSize = 128;

    mic.connect(analyser);

    var bufferLength = analyser.frequencyBinCount;
```

```
    var frequencyData = new Uint8Array(bufferLength);

    // assume some canvas and ctx objects already loaded and bound
to the DOM
    var WIDTH = canvas.width;
    var HEIGHT = canvas.height;
    var lastTime = 0;

    visualize(e);

    function visualize(now) {
        // we'll slow down the render speed so it looks smoother
        requestAnimationFrame(draw);
        if (now - lastTime >= 200) {
            ctx.clearRect(0, 0, WIDTH, HEIGHT);
            analyser.getByteFrequencyData(frequencyData);

            var barWidth = (WIDTH / bufferLength) * 2.5;
            var x = 0;

            [].forEach.call(frequencyData, function (barHeight) {
                ctx.fillStyle = 'rgb(50, ' + (barHeight + 100) + ',
50)';
                ctx.fillRect(x, HEIGHT - barHeight / 1, barWidth,
barHeight / 1);
                x += barWidth + 1;
            });

            lastTime = now;
        }
    }
};
```

Working with a video is equally simple, but it does require, as you would expect, that a camera to be connected to your computer. If you make the request to `getUserMedia` with a set video constraint, but no camera is present, the error callback will be executed and the `NavigatorUserMediaError` object will sent as the argument:

```
navigator.webkitGetUserMedia({video: true}, function(stream){
    // ...
}, function(e){
    // e => NavigatorUserMediaError {
    //              constraintName: '',
    //              message: '',
    //              name: 'DevicesNotFoundError'
    //          }
});
```

On the other hand, when a video device is accessible, we can stream it to a video element in the most simple manner by setting its `src` attribute to a `objectUrl`, which is pointing to the stream source that we acquire from the user media:

```
var video = document.createElement('video');
video.setAttribute('controls', true);
video.setAttribute('autoplay', true);

document.body.appendChild(video);

var constraints = {
    video: true
};

function allowCallback(stream){
    video.src = window.URL.createObjectURL(stream);
}

function denyCallback(e){
    console.error('Could not access media devices', e);
}

navigator.webkitGetUserMedia(constraints, allowCallback,
denyCallback);
```

Summary

This chapter took us forward in time, giving us a glimpse of the latest HTML5 APIs that we can incorporate into our multiplayer games. These APIs include the Fullscreen mode, gamepad, media capture, and WebRTC. With these powerful additional features, your games will be that much more engaging and fun to play.

However, the one takeaway point from the entire discussion is that all of the APIs that were described in this chapter are still in the early drafting stages; therefore, they can be subjected to drastic interface changes, or they can be deprecated as well. In the meantime, be sure to add the appropriate vendor prefixes to each API and look out for any one-off browser quirks or implementation differences.

In the next chapter, we'll conclude our journey through the wonderful world of multiplayer game development in JavaScript by discussing security vulnerabilities that are associated with network gaming. We'll describe common techniques to minimize opportunities for cheating, thus providing a fair and adequate playing experience.

Adding Security and Fair Play

6

Although we're only now talking about security, the main takeaway from this chapter is that security should be baked into your games. Just like other types of software, you can't just go in after the fact, slap in a few security features and expect the product to be bullet proof. However, since the primary focus of this book was not security, I think we can be justified in not bringing up the subject until the very last chapter.

In this chapter, we will discuss the following principles and concepts:

- Common security vulnerabilities in web-based applications
- Using Npm and Bower to add extra security to your games
- Making games more secure and less prone to cheating

Common security vulnerabilities

If you're coming to game development from one of the many other areas of software development, you will be pleased to know that securing a game is not much different than securing any other type of software. Treating a game like any other type of software that needs security, especially like a distributed and networked one, will help you to put in place the proper measures that will help you to protect your software.

In this section, we will cover a few of the most basic and fundamental security vulnerabilities in web-based applications (including games) as well as ways to protect against them. However, we will not delve too deeply (or at all) into more complicated networking security topics and scenarios, such as social engineering, denial of service attacks, securing user accounts, storing sensitive data properly, protecting virtual assets, and so on.

Encryption over the wire

The first vulnerability about which you should be aware of is that sending data from your server to your clients leaves the data exposed for others to see. Monitoring network traffic is almost as easy as walking and chewing gum at the same time, even though not everyone is skilled enough to do either of these things.

Here's a common scenario that you might require your players to go through while they play (or prepare to play) your game:

- The player enters a username and password in order to be authorized into your game
- Your server validates the login information
- The player is then allowed to continue on and play the game

If the initial HTTP request sent to the server by the player is not encrypted, then anyone who was looking at the network packets would know the user credentials and your player's account would be compromised.

The easiest solution is to transmit any such data over HTTPS. While using HTTPS won't solve all of one's security problems, it does provide us with a fairly certain guarantee, which includes the following points:

- The server responding to the client request would be who it says it is
- The data received by both the server and the client would not have been tampered with
- Anyone looking at the data wouldn't be able to read it in plain text

Since HTTPS packets are encrypted, anyone monitoring the network will need to decrypt each packet in order to know data that it contained, thus making it a safe way to send one's password to the server.

Just as there is no such thing as a *free meal*, there is also no such thing as free encryption and decryption. This means that by using HTTPS you will incur some measurable performance penalty. What this penalty actually is and how negligible it will be is highly dependent on a series of factors. The key is to evaluate your specific case and determine where exactly the use of HTTPS would be too expensive in terms of performance.

However, remember that at a very minimum, trading off performance for security is worth the cost when the value of the data is greater than the extra performance. It is possible that you may not be able to transmit thousands of players' positions and velocities per second over HTTPS because of the associated latency this would cause. However, each individual user will not be logging in very often after one initial authentication, so forcing at least that to be secure is certainly something nobody can afford to go without.

Script injection

The base principle behind this vulnerability is that your script takes user input as text (data) and evaluates it as code in an execution context. A typical use case for this is as follows:

- The game asks for the user to enter his/her name
- A malicious user enters code
- The game optionally saves that text for future use
- The game eventually uses that code in an execution context

In the case of web-based application, or more specifically with JavaScript being executed in a browser, the vicious input might be a string of HTML and the execution context the DOM. One particular feature of the DOM API is its ability to set a string as an element's HTML content. The browser takes that string and turns it into live HTML, just like any other HTML document that is rendered in some server.

The following code snippet is an example of an application that asks for a user's nickname, then displays it on the upper-right corner of the screen. This game may also save the player's name in a database and attempt to render that string with the player's name in other parts of the game as well:

```
/**
 * @param {Object} player
 */
function setPlayerName(player){
    var nameIn = document.getElementById('nameIn');
    var nameOut = document.getElementById('nameOut');

    player.name = nameIn.value;
```

```
        // Warning: here be danger!
        nameOut.innerHTML = player.name;
}
```

For the casual developer, this seems like a rather lovely greeting to a player who is getting ready to enjoy your platform game. Provided that the user enters an actual name with no HTML characters in it, all will be well.

However, if the user decides to call himself something like `<script src="http://my-website.com/my-script.js"></script>` instead and we don't sanitize that string in order to remove characters that would make the string a valid HTML, the application could become compromised.

The two possible ways to exploit this vulnerability as a user are to alter the client's experience (for example, by entering an HTML string that makes the name blink or downloads and plays an arbitrary MP3 file), or to input an HTML string that downloads and executes JavaScript files that alter the main game script and interacts with the game's server in malicious ways.

To make matters worse, if we're not careful with protecting against other vulnerabilities, this security loophole can be exploited in conjunction with other vulnerabilities, further compounding the damage that can be done by an evil player:

Server validation

Depending on how we process and use input from our users on the server, we can compromise the server and other assets by trusting the user with unsanitized input. However, just making sure that the input is generally valid is not enough.

For example, at some point you will tell the server where the player is, how fast and in which direction he or she is moving, and possibly which buttons are being pressed. In case we need to inform the server about the player's position, we would first verify that the client game has submitted a valid number:

```
// src/server/input-handler.js

socket.on(gameEvents.server_userPos, function(data){
    var position = {
        x: parseFloat(data.x),
        y: parseFloat(data.y)
    };

    if (isNaN(position.x) || isNan(position.y) {
        // Discard input
    }

    // ...
});
```

Now that we know that the user hasn't hacked the game to send in malicious code instead of their actual location vector, we can perform calculations on it and update the rest of the game state. Or, can we?

If the user sends invalid floats for their position, for example (assuming that we're working with floating point numbers in this case), we can simply discard the input or perform a specific action in response to their attempt to enter invalid values. However, what would we do if the user sends an incorrect location vector?

It could be that the player is moving along from the left side of the screen to the right. First, the server receives the player's coordinates showing where the player really is, then the player reports to being slightly further to the right and a little closer to a fiery pit. Suppose that the fastest the player can possibly move is, say, 5 pixels per frame. Then, how would we know whether the player truly did jump over and across the fiery pit in one frame (which is an impossible move) or whether the player cheated, if all we know is that the player sent a valid vector saying {x: 2484, y: 4536}?

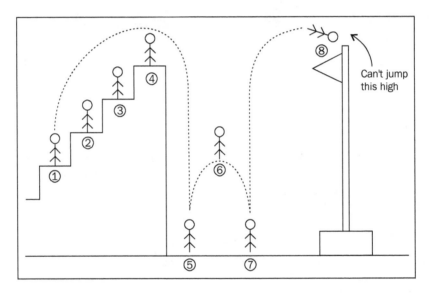

The key principle here is to validate whether the input is valid. Note that we're talking about validating and not sanitizing user input although the latter is also indispensable and goes hand in hand with the former.

In its simplest form, one solution to the previous problem with a player reporting a fake position is that we could simply keep track of the last reported position and compare it to the one that is received next. For a more complex solution, we could keep track of the several previous positions and take a look at how the player is moving.

```javascript
var PlayerPositionValidator = function(maxDx, maxDy) {
    this.maxDx = maxDx;
    this.maxDy = maxDy;
    this.positions = [];
};

PlayerPositionValidator.prototype.addPosition = function(x, y){
    var pos = {
        x: x,
        y: y
    };

    this.positions.push(pos);
};

PlayerPositionValidator.prototype.checkLast = function(x, y){
    var pos = this.positions[this.positions.length - 1];

    return Math.abs(pos.x - x) <= this.maxDx
        && Math.abs(pos.y - y) <= this.maxDy;
};
```

The above class keeps track of the maximum vertical and horizontal displacement that a player can possibly have in a frame (or however often the server validates a new user position). By associating an instance of it to a specific player, we can add new incoming positions as well as check it against the last one received to determine whether it's greater than the maximum possible displacement.

A more complicated case to check for and validate against would be making sure that the player does not report potentially expired events or attributes (such as temporary power ups, and so on), or invalid input state (for example, the player is already in the air, but is suddenly reporting that a jump was initiated).

To make matters even more complex, there is another case that we need to be aware of, which is very difficult to check. So far, as we've discussed, the solution to combat against players trying to manipulate game state is to use the authoritative server's power to overrule clients' actions. However, as we will discuss in the next section, there's one family of problems that even an authoritative server can't really prevent or recover from.

Artificial intelligence

It is one thing to detect a player who is trying to cheat because the reported moves are impossible to make (for example, moving too fast or firing a weapon that is not available in a given level in the game). An entirely different thing, however, is to try to detect a cheater because he or she is playing too well. This is a possible vulnerability that we can face if the vicious player is a bot playing perfect games against honest humans who are trying to compete.

The solution to this issue is as complex as the problem. Assuming that you want to prevent bots from competing against humans, how can you possibly determine that a series of inputs are coming from another software instead of a human player? Presumably, although every move will be a legal one, the level of accuracy will likely be orders of magnitude higher than everyone else's.

Unfortunately, implementations in code demonstrating ways to combat this class of problems is beyond the scope of this book. In general, you will want to use various heuristics to determine whether a series of moves is too perfect.

Building secure games and applications

Now that we've discussed some basic things to watch out for, and the things you shouldn't perform in your games; we will now take a look at some simple concepts that we cannot leave out of the game.

Again, most of these concepts apply to web development in general, so those of you coming from that world would feel right at home.

Authoritative server

Hopefully, it is clear by now that the key to having trustworthy information is to ensure that the source of that information is trustworthy. In our case, we rely on the game server to listen to all of the clients and then determine what is the truth about the current game state.

Should you ever find yourself in a situation where you are considering not using a server-client model for your multiplayer game in favor of some alternative format, one thing you should always keep in mind is that the security like that can be obtained by putting an authority between two players. Even if a single player decides to manipulate and cheat his or her own game client, the authoritative game server can ensure that other players still have an equal and fair experience.

While not every game format calls for an authoritative game server, you should have a really good reason for not using one when your specific game could be implemented using one.

Session-based gameplay

One of the benefits of modern browsers is that they feature very powerful JavaScript engines that enable us to do so much in the client with straight JavaScript. As a result, there is a lot of heavy lifting that we can offload from the server to the client.

For example, suppose we want to save the current player's game state. This would include the player's current position, health, lives, score, etc., as well as virtual currency, achievements, and more.

One approach would be to encode all of this information and store it in the user's machine. The problem with this is that the user could alter the saved file, and we would never know about it. Thus, a common step in this process is to create a hash of the final saved file, then later use this same hash to ensure that the game's saved file hasn't been altered.

> What is the difference between a `hash` and an `encryption`?
>
> Perhaps, you have heard both the terms being used interchangeably, but they're actually very different concepts. While both are often associated with security, this is about the only similarity that they share.
>
> A hash function maps a string of some arbitrary length to a string of some fixed length. Given the same input string, the same output hash is always returned. The main feature of a hash function is that the mapping is unidirectional, which means that the function cannot be reverted in order to get the original input from its output.
>
> For example, the `Rodrigo Silveira` input string would map to something like `73cade4e8326`. Hashing this output string would return something completely different from itself or the original input.
>
> Encryption, on the other hand, is a way to convert some input string into a different representation of that string, but with the ability to reverse (or undo) the function and get back the original input string.
>
> For example, if you use Caesar's cipher (named after the powerful Roman general, not the Brazilian soccer player) to encrypt the Rodrigo Silveira string with a shift value of 3 (which means that every character in the input text is shifted by 3 letters), you'd get the output as `Urguljr Vloyhlud`. — that is, the third character after the letter `R`, which is the letter `U`, and so on. If we apply a shift value of `-3` to the output string would give us back the original string.
>
> In short, for all practical purposes, a hash cannot be reversed while an encryption can.

However, if we also store the hash with the client, then all they would need to do after altering the game save file is to recalculate the hash, and we'd be right back where we started.

A better approach would be to calculate the hash on the server, store the hash in the server, and associate it with the player through some user account system. This way, if any tampering is done to the locally stored file, the server can verify it using the hash to which only it had access.

There are also cases when you might want to store API keys or other unique objects of this nature with the client. Again, the key principle here is that anything that touches the client is now under the control of your enemy and cannot be trusted.

Thus, the main takeaway from this section is to always store keys and other sensitive pieces of data like it inside the server and associate and proxy them to and for the player through session tokens.

Security through obscurity

While obscurity is not a form of security, it does add a layer of complexity that slows down the truly determined (and skilled) malicious user and filters out most other evil doers who would otherwise attempt to exploit your game.

In web development, the most common way to obscure your game is by running your final source code through some JavaScript compiler that safely renames variables and function names as well as rewrites code in a way that is equivalent to your original input code but performs the same tasks.

For example, you might have code like the following one, which can be exploited very easily by the player by changing the value of some variables using their browser's JavaScript console:

```javascript
Gameloop.prototype.update = function(){
    Players.forEach(function(player){
        hero.bullets.filter(function(bullet){
            if (player.intersects(bullet)) {
                player.takeDamage(bullet.power);
                hero.score += bullet.hp;

                return false
            }

            return true;
        });
    });

    // ...
};
```

We don't have to look too closely at the previous function to realize that only bullets that hit other players in this fictitious game gives damage to each player and increase our own score. Thus, writing a function to replace that is trivial or at least modifying its important parts to the same end can be just as easy.

Now, running that function through a tool such as Google's closure compiler (to know more on closure compiler, refer to `https://developers.google.com/closure/compiler/`) would output something similar to the following, which is clearly not impossible to manipulate but is certainly not as trivial:

```
_l.prototype.U=function(){c.forEach(function(e){i.a.filter(
function(o){return e.R(o)?(e.a4(o.d),i.$+=o.F,!1):!0})})};
```

Most JavaScript obfuscator programs will rename function names, variables, and attributes as well as remove unnecessary whitespace, brackets, and semicolons, making the output program very compact and hard to read. Some additional benefits of using these programs prior to deploying your code include having smaller files that you'll end up sending to your clients (thus saving bandwidth), and in the case of closure compiler, it rewrites parts of your code so that the output is optimal.

The key takeaway from this section is that adding layers of complexity to your code makes it that much more secure, and at the very least, helps you to get rid of some class of attackers. Much like adding a camera above your front door won't necessarily eliminate possible intruders from breaking in, it sure does go a long ways in scaring unwelcome visitors.

"Remember, however, that obscurity is not security at all. It is trivial to deobfuscate an obfuscated JavaScript program (even compiled programs can be easily decompiled back into partial source code). You should never rely on obfuscation and obscurity alone as a solid form of security. Obfuscating your deployed application should be a final touch to an already secure system, especially considering the major benefits of obfuscation, as mentioned previously.

Reinventing the wheel

Like most problems in computer science, someone has already found a solution and converted it into code. In this regard, we have been particularly benefited by so many generous (and very smart) programmers who distribute their solutions through open source projects.

In this section, I invite you to look for existing solutions instead of taking the time to write your own. Although coding complex solutions to interesting problems is always fun (unless, maybe, your boss is pressing you about an upcoming deadline), you may find that your efforts are better invested in making your actual game.

As we've discussed in *Chapter 2*, *Setting Up the Environment*, having access to the Node.js ecosystem gives you a lot of leverage to find, use, and eventually share great tools for many problems that you may come across when you develop your games.

In sticking with the theme of security and fair play, what follows is a list of common tools that we can use through **Npm** and **Bower** (as well as **Grunt** and **Gulp**) to help us deal with security in our games.

Npm install validator

This module allows you to validate and sanitize data very effortlessly. You can use validator on the server as well as in the browser. Simply require the module in and call its various methods on your input:

```
var validator = require('validator');

validator.isEmail('foo@bar.com'); //=> true
validator.isBase64(inStr);
validator.isHexColor(inStr);
validator.isJSON(inStr);
```

There are methods for checking just about any type of data or format as well as to sanitize data so that you don't have to write your own functions for it.

Npm install js-sha512

This simple module is used to hash strings using a variety of algorithms. To use the library as a standalone library in the browser, you can also import it using Bower:

```
bower install js-sha512
```

To use `js-sha512`, simply `require` it to the desired hashing function and send it the string to be hashed:

```
sha512 = require('js-sha512').sha512;
sha384 = require('js-sha512').sha384;

var s512 = sha512('Rodrigo Silveira');
var s384 = sha384('Rodrigo Silveira');
```

Npm install closure compiler

As mentioned previously, Google's closure compiler is a very powerful software that was open-sourced several years ago. The benefits that can be gained by using the compiler extend far beyond simply wanting to obfuscate code. For example, the compiler allows you to annotate your JavaScript code with data types, which the compiler can then look at and tell you whether a variable violates that contract:

```
/**
 * @param {HTMLImageElement} img
 * @constructor
 */
var Sprite = function(img) {
    this.img = img;
};


/**
 * @param {CanvasRenderingContext2D} ctx
 */
Sprite.prototype.draw = function(ctx) {
    // ...
};


/**
 * @param {number} x
 * @param {number} y
 * @param {Sprite} sprite
 * @constructor
 */
var Player = function(x, y, sprite) {
    this.x = x;
    this.y = y;
    this.sprite = sprite;
};
```

In the given sample code , you will note that the `Player` and `Sprite` constructor functions are annotated with the `@constructor` annotation. When the closure compiler sees the code calling these functions without a new operator, it will deduce that the code is being exercised in a way different from how it was intended and raise a compilation error so that you can fix the bad code. In addition, if you attempt to instantiate a `Player`, for example, and the value sent to the constructor is not a pair of numbers followed by an instance of the `Sprite` class, the compiler will bring this to your attention so that your code can be corrected.

The easiest way to use the closure compiler is to lean on Grunt or Gulp and install the equivalent build task for closure. The popular solutions are as follows:

```
// For Grunt users:
npm install grunt-closure-compiler

// If you prefer Gulp:
npm install gulp-closure-compiler
```

Fair play and the user experience

So far in this chapter, we have discussed many different aspects of security, all of which were aimed at providing fair play to your users. Although we can do the best we can to secure our servers, intellectual property, user data, and other players, at the end of the day, the attacker will always be at an advantage.

Especially in multiplayer games, where dozens, if not hundreds or thousands of different players will be enjoying your game at the same time, you may come to a point where attempting to secure a player against himself is not a good investment of time or other resources. For example, if an isolated player wishes to cheat his or her way into jumping higher than the game allows or change a save game in order to reflect extra lives, then you may be better off just letting that player proceed with the hack on his or her own client. Just be absolutely sure that none of the other players are affected by it.

The key takeaway from this section as well as from the entire chapter is that user experience is the king. Even more so when multiple players are sharing a game world looking for a fun time and one of these players is only looking for a way to ruin it for everyone; you must make sure that no matter what happens, the other players can continue to play.

Summary

With this chapter, we wrapped up the discussion on multiplayer game development although it covers a topic that must be a deep part of your game development from the beginning. Remember that security cannot simply be added at the end of the project; instead, it must be built in deliberately with the rest of the software.

We saw some of the most basic security vulnerabilities in browser-based games as well as common ways to protect your games against them. We also talked about a few techniques that no serious game should be built without. Finally, we looked at how to implement some of these techniques using existing open source tools through Node's Npm.

In conclusion, now that you have cleared the last level of this journey of learning the basics of multiplayer game development in JavaScript, I want you to know that as exciting as this might have been, your journey is not quite over yet. *Thank you for reading, but the princess is in another castle!* You must now get busy with writing the next multiplayer game that will take all players through a journey full of fun, entertainment, and real-time awesomeness. Game over!

Index

Symbols

/BoardServer.js class 21
/Player.js class 20
/public/js/app.js class 25, 26
/public/js/Board.js class 24, 25
/server.js class 22-24

A

artificial intelligence 148
Asynchronous Module Definition (AMD)
  URL 38
authoritative server
  about 148
  game client, updating 71-74
  game server interface 69, 70
  implementing 69

B

benefits, client-server networking
  centralization 7
  less work for the client 7
  separation of concerns 7
benefits, peer-to-peer networking
  fast data transmission 4
  reliability 4
  simpler setup 4
Bower
  URL 43
  used, for managing frontend
     packages 43, 44
  using 152

Browserify
about 39, 44-46
URL 44

C

clients
  synchronizing 96-99
client-server networking
  about 5, 6
  benefits 7
  drawbacks 7, 8
client-side code 39
client-side Socket.io 88, 89
CommonJS
  about 33-38
  URL 33
Composer 40

D

datagrams 9

E

ECMA 13
encryption
  about 142
  versus hash 149
error correction
  about 103
  scenarios 104-111
Express framework 53
Express.js
  about 54
  URL 54

Thank you for buying
Multiplayer Game Development with HTML5

About Packt Publishing

Packt, pronounced 'packed', published its first book, *Mastering phpMyAdmin for Effective MySQL Management*, in April 2004, and subsequently continued to specialize in publishing highly focused books on specific technologies and solutions.

Our books and publications share the experiences of your fellow IT professionals in adapting and customizing today's systems, applications, and frameworks. Our solution-based books give you the knowledge and power to customize the software and technologies you're using to get the job done. Packt books are more specific and less general than the IT books you have seen in the past. Our unique business model allows us to bring you more focused information, giving you more of what you need to know, and less of what you don't.

Packt is a modern yet unique publishing company that focuses on producing quality, cutting-edge books for communities of developers, administrators, and newbies alike. For more information, please visit our website at www.packtpub.com.

About Packt Open Source

In 2010, Packt launched two new brands, Packt Open Source and Packt Enterprise, in order to continue its focus on specialization. This book is part of the Packt Open Source brand, home to books published on software built around open source licenses, and offering information to anybody from advanced developers to budding web designers. The Open Source brand also runs Packt's Open Source Royalty Scheme, by which Packt gives a royalty to each open source project about whose software a book is sold.

Writing for Packt

We welcome all inquiries from people who are interested in authoring. Book proposals should be sent to author@packtpub.com. If your book idea is still at an early stage and you would like to discuss it first before writing a formal book proposal, then please contact us; one of our commissioning editors will get in touch with you.

We're not just looking for published authors; if you have strong technical skills but no writing experience, our experienced editors can help you develop a writing career, or simply get some additional reward for your expertise.

[PACKT] PUBLISHING

Learning Cocos2d-JS Game Development

ISBN: 978-1-78439-007-5   Paperback: 188 pages

Learn to create robust and engaging cross-platform HTML5 games using Cocos2d-JS

1. Create HTML5 games running both on desktop and mobile devices, played with both mouse and touch controls.

2. Add advanced features such as realistic physics, particle effects, scrolling, tweaking, sound effects, background music, and more to your games.

3. Build exciting cross-platform games and build a memory game, an endless runner and a physics-driven game.

HTML5 Game Development [Video]

ISBN: 978-1-84969-588-6   Duration: 01:58 hours

Build two HTML5 games in two hours with these fast-paced beginner-friendly videos

1. Create two simple yet elegant games in HTML5.

2. Build games that run on both desktops and mobile browsers.

3. Presented in a modular approach, with elegant code and illustrated concepts to help you learn quickly.

Please check **www.PacktPub.com** for information on our titles